"A complete and thorough guide to structuring a script and as helpful a 'how-to' book as one could ask."

Jean Firstenberg, Director,
The American Film Institute

"A Wonderful, most useful book. It will never become a movie, but I daresay it might help a great many good ones to be written."

Larry Gelbart, writer,
Tootsie, "M*A*S*H"

"Very complete, very comprehensive, it covers all the bases. It aims for the highest purpose of what screenwriting is about—the art of storytelling."

Robert Wise, President,
Academy of Motion Picture
Arts and Sciences, film director

"A practical and clear resource of value for students en route to becoming screenwriters."

Margaret Mehring, Director,
Filmic Writing Program,
School of Cinema-Television, USC

MAKING A GOOD SCRIPT GREAT

Other books by Linda Seger:

Creating Unforgettable Characters

The Art of Adaptation: Turning Fact and Fiction into Film

From Script to Screen: The Collaborative Art of Filmmaking
(co-authored with Edward Jay Whetmore)

MAKING A GOOD SCRIPT GREAT

2nd Edition

LINDA SEGER

SAMUEL FRENCH ■ Hollywood
New York ■ London ■ Toronto

Acknowledgment is made to the following for permission to
reproduce the material indicated

MCA Publishing Rights for excerpts from *Back to the Future,* copyright
© Universal Pictures, a division of Universal City Studios, Inc., courtesy of MCA Publishing Rights, a division of MCA, Inc.; MCA Publishing RIghts and Peter Benchley for excerpts from *Jaws,* copyright ©
Universal Pictures, a division of Universal Pictures, a division of
Universal City Studios, Inc., Courtesy of MCA Publishing Rights, a
division of MCA, Inc.; Excerpts from *Witness* © Paramount Pictures;
Columbia Pictures, Don McGuire, Larry Gelbart, and Murray Schisgal
for excerpts from *Tootsie*; Horizon Management, Inc. for excerpts from
the *African Queen.*

First Edition
10 9 8 7 6 5 4 3 2 1

Library of Congress Cataloging-in-Publication Date

Linda Seger
Making a good script great / Linga Seger. —2nd ed.
p. cm.
Includes index.
1. Motion picture authorship. I. Title.
PN1996.S384 1994   808.2'3—dc20   94-32338
ISBN: 0-573-69921-6

Cover design by Hal Siegel. Adapted for the second edition by Arthead.

Printed and bound in the United States of America

Published and distributed by
Samuel French Trade
7623 Sunset Boulevard
Hollywood, CA 90046

To my mentor,
Dr. Wayne Rood

Contents

Acknowledgments

With many thanks . . .

To Dr. Leonard Felder for the title, and for editing the second edition of this book, and to Cynthia Vartan, for editing the first edition of this book,

To Dara Marks for honest feedback, encouragement, and constant support,

To my readers for this second edition—Sharon Cobb, Carolyn Miller, and Treva Silverman—and the readers for the first edition—Mary Beth Gaik, Mark Gerzon, and Lindsay Smith. I thank you all for your insights, input, and all your help,

To Cathleen Loeser and Chris Vogler for help on Chapter Six,

To Bill Kelley And David Bombyk for information and two memorable meals as we discussed *Witness*. And to Pamela Wallace and Earl Wallace, who filled me in on additional information for this second edition,

To Columbia Pictures and Larry Gelbart, Don McGuire, and Murray Schisgal for permission to quote from *Tootsie,*

To Horizon Films for permission to quote from *The African Queen,*

To Universal/MCA and Peter Benchley for permission to quote from *Jaws,* and to Universal and Amblin Entertainment, along with Bob Gale and Robert Zemeckis, for permission to quote from *Back to the Future,*

To Paramount Pictures for permission to quote from *Witness,*

To George Lucas and Lucasfilm Ltd. for permission to quote from *Raiders of the Lost Ark,*

And always to my husband, Peter Le Var, for constant affection, a loving spirit, and for those terrific back rubs that kept me writing.

Author's Preface

When I wrote the first edition of *Making a Good Script Great*, there were a number of screenwriting books on the market, but none that dealt with the important rewriting process. I chose to focus on rewriting. However, as readers began to give me feedback, I learned that my book was helpful to beginning writers who wanted to know how to write a script as well as to Academy Award-winning writers who were encountering problems while rewriting. But it was not giving the readers all the information they needed to create that script from the first draft through the shooting draft. What was missing in the first edition was the first step in the process of writing—gathering ideas—and another important step in the writing—creating the scene. I decided that it was time to do a new edition. Since clearly the book was helping a great number of writers, I wanted to make it as complete as possible, but not to fix what wasn't broken.

The second edition is essentially the same book as the first edition, with the addition of two chapters, some updated examples from films, and some additional information within the chapters. In this edition, you'll find an expanded discussion about theme, credit sequences, the midpoint scene, and montages. I have retained the use of my main examples from three

films that clearly stand the test of time: *The African Queen,*
Witness, and *Tootsie.* In the first edition, I was not allowed to
quote from *Witness.* For this edition, Paramount Studios has
kindly given me permission to quote from the script, which
makes it possible to expand on many of the concepts from the
first edition.

I thank all my readers who have enjoyed the first edition
and hope you continue to enjoy *Making a Good Script Great.*

Introduction

Making a great script is not just a matter of having a good idea. Nor is it a matter of just putting your good idea down on paper. In scriptwriting, more than any other form of writing, it's not just the writing, it's also the rewriting that makes a good script great.

The underlying principles for writing a script are essentially the same in rewriting. If you're writing your first script, this book will help develop your skills for telling a compelling and dramatic story. If you're a veteran screenwriter, this book will articulate the skills you know intuitively. And if you are currently stuck on a rewrite, this book will help you analyze and solve the problems to get your script back "on track."

This book will take you through the process, from the first spark of an idea through the rewriting process. When you begin your script, you need to know how to organize your ideas, how to create a compelling story, how to make your characters dimensional and worthy of our company for two hours. But you'll also need to know how to rewrite the script when you're finished— because if you write, you will rewrite. That's the nature of the business. Unless you're a writer who writes "for yourself" and puts your scripts in a box in the garage, you will find yourself rewriting—again and again. First, you will do it to get your first draft "just right." Then your friends will have a few suggestions, and you'll rewrite "just to make it a little better." Your agent will have some suggestions about how to make it more marketable, and you'll incorporate those. The producer and development executive will want you to do another rewrite so that they can "put their stamp" on it. And the actors will have ideas about "what works for them" and want you to give them "just a little bit more."

Now this is all well and good, provided you know what to rewrite and provided that every rewrite improves the script. Unfortunately, this rarely happens. Many people feel like the man who decided to become a writer because he saw so much bad writing on television and in film. "Certainly I can do better than that!" he said. After submitting his script to a producer who turned him down, he protested, "But it's much better than anything else I've seen!" "Of course," said the producer. "Anyone can write better than that. The trick is to write so brilliantly that after everyone ruins it in rewrites, it's still watchable."

And it's true. Many scripts get worse and worse in the rewrite process. The farther they get from the original inspirational source, the more muddled they become. They begin to lose their magic. By the fifth rewrite, beats drop out of the script and certain elements no longer make sense. By the twelfth rewrite, the story is completely different, and no one wants to do the film anymore.

The solution might seem to be "Don't rewrite!" It is, unfortunately, not an alternative. Most scripts, even with all the creativity and magic that a writer puts into the first draft, don't work. Many of them are overwritten. They're simply too long to make a good, salable film. Many writers forget something in the creativity of the moment—to pay off a clue, to complete a character through-line, to finish off a subplot. Some of them have a germ of an idea running through the script that only appears as the writer gets deeper and deeper into the story. Without a rewrite, all of those elements would remain unworkable.

So what's the answer? Or is there one? The answer doesn't sound all that difficult: Only rewrite what doesn't work and leave the rest alone. Doing this is the problem, because it often means working against the temptation to do more and more. It means not getting carried away by some new and different idea that's exciting but doesn't fix the problem. It means not fixing the entire script, but only fixing what doesn't work. It means holding back on a new creative stamp because the writer's original creative stamp is "just fine, thank you." And it means that suggestions are designed to get the script "on track," not off.

So how is this done? This book is designed to discuss just that. It's designed to discuss what "on track" means and to look at concepts that can be applied to a good script to make it better. It's designed to teach you how to write and rewrite quickly and efficiently, while keeping the magic for that important last draft—the shooting script.

My career as a script consultant has focused almost exclusively on how to get the script on track so that problems are solved and the original creativity is preserved. I've worked on hundreds of feature and television scripts. I've worked on miniseries, television movies, dramatic series, and sitcoms, and on horror films, action-adventures, comedies, dramas, and fantasies.The challenge is always the same—how to make the next draft work. This is the same whether I work with writers, producers, directors, or executives. Together, our job is to analyze the problems, define the concepts, and find the solutions that will create a workable draft. I've worked with many of the most creative and successful people in the business and realized that problems in writing and rewriting happen with everyone, no matter how experienced the writer is.

Usually, the difficulties occur because the problems aren't well-defined or analyzed before starting the rewrite. As a result the producer might say, "It's the second act," so a rewrite is done to fix the second act. Then the director says, "Now I see we have a problem with the main character," so another rewrite focuses on the main character. Next, another rewrite occurs to fix the subplot problem. And the subplot rewrite throws the main plot off track, so another rewrite tries to fix that.

Since the script works as a whole, naturally the changes to one part of the script affect the changes in another. My job as a script consultant is to identify and analyze those problems before the rewrite and work with the creators to make sure that all the problems get solved. I've discovered that the process of rewriting a script is not just an amorphous, magical, "maybe-it-works, maybe-it-doesn't" kind of process. There are specific elements that make a good script great, elements that can be consciously analyzed and improved.

Naturally, since every script is unique, the problems of every script are different. It's not possible to write a book that you can follow point by point to create the perfect script. The creative process is not a paint-by-the-numbers process, and this book is not designed to give you some simple rules and formulas to apply by rote.

However, in my experience with scripts, I see the same kinds of problems occur again and again. Problems in exposition. Problems with momentum. Problems with an insufficiently developed idea. Problems that can make the difference between a sale and another rejection letter, between commercial success or box-office failure.

To understand how these problems have been solved in great scripts, I'll be discussing some of the most workable and satisfying films. From the first edition of this book, I have retained many of the same examples, concentrating on the films of *Witness, The African Queen,* and *Tootsie.* All three of these films stand the test of time and remain excellent teaching films, as well as entertaining films, that you can watch again and again. If you simply study these films, you will learn a lot about the art and craft of writing. I also continue to use examples from *Jaws, Star Wars,* and *Back to the Future,* which remains one of the best films for understanding foreshadowing and payoff. I have added an example from *Raiders of the Lost Ark* and expanded my discussion to some more recent films; *Unforgiven,*

Schindler's List, and *The Fugitive.* And I mention a number of other films with less detail, including *Gone With the Wind Fatal Attraction, Ghostbusters,* and *Ruthless People.* All of these have done well at the box office and have achieved some sort of critical acclaim. And these films are high on my list of good teaching films. They're well structured with strong dimensional characters and a well worked-out idea. But they are not formula films. They're creative, artistic, and well crafted. If you haven't seen these films, you can rent them on videocassette. You'll want to be familiar with them, since each chapter will deal in some depth with particular elements in these films. And, of course, while discovering why they work and how they work, you will also be entertained.

It is my belief that it takes both a good write, and a good rewrite, to create a film that entertains, has something to say, and is of high quality. With some creativity and a good idea you can get a good script. This book is about making that good script great!

Part One

Story Structure

Chapter One

Gathering Ideas

You're a writer. You've got a great idea for a film. You think it's as good as *E.T.* It's as original as *Ghostbusters,* as intimate as *Driving Miss Daisy*, it's got some great *Die Hard* action, and it pushes the genre like *Unforgiven.* You know it's not just the idea but the execution that counts. You want to do it right. Where do you begin?

Or you're an executive. You saw an article that gave you some ideas for a story. You want to get your thoughts down before hiring a writer. You want to be clear and you want to create a workable storyline. How do you do it?

You're a director. You've never written a script before, but you have a storyline that's been pushing at you for a year or two. You want to get the story down in treatment or script form—then maybe you'll find a writer to collaborate with you. How do you start?

Rarely do ideas appear full-blown. Most scripts begin with a spark. A snippet of images. Perhaps it begins with a situation you want to explore. Maybe it starts with a character you've known or imagined. It could be parts of a story that pull at you, demanding to be told. It might be as small as a one-line idea— "Something about a circus." It might be as big as an epic—"My grandfather told me stories about fighting in the Russian Revolution." But somewhere between the idea and 120 pages of script, the idea will need to take form. The story needs to be shaped, fleshed out with characters, built with images and emotions, and woven through with ideas. How it's done will determine whether the screenplay is a muddle, merely competent, or a brilliant piece of art.

As with any other art form, writing a script begins with a certain degree of chaos. Ideas are half-baked. Storylines can get bogged down at any point. Characters might seem inconsistent, one-dimensional, too predictable, or too much like a character you've seen a hundred times before. You don't know yet what you have, and you don't know what you're getting.

The process of writing is a process of moving from chaos to order. How quickly you move will depend on how fast you write, how much you know about the process and craft of writing, how disciplined you are, the difficulty of your idea, the amount of research you need to do, and how much you value your own creative process. Some of you may be fast-thinking, organized, with ideas spilling out as quickly as you can write them down. Others may need time to mull, season. consider, ruminate over ideas. There is no right way to be creative. There is no one process that will work for everyone.

GETTING THE IDEA

Where do ideas come from? The world is brimming with fascinating stories, dramatic characters, and intriguing ideas and issues. Part of your training as a writer consists of finding the clues, hints, small threads that can form the basis for a great script. Many writers find ideas from newspaper articles. The newspaper is filled with conflict, drama, dynamic characters, and important issues. Your own immediate family—good or bad—contains a myriad of situations that can be explored. Friendships, marriages, problems at work—whether from your own life or situations you've heard about—can be used. And your dreams, fantasies, hopes, goals—as well as your failures, disappointments, and betrayals—are all grist for the mill of your creativity.

Many situations, when coupled with a good dose of imagination, can lead to new ideas. You might ask, "What if I had married him?" "What could have happened if I had taken the job in the Middle East?" "Suppose I had gone to that boarding school?"

Many writers keep file folders filled with possible stories. Some have hundreds of one-liners on their computer. Others have notes scattered about. Eventually one story begins to call, wanting to be told.

ORDERING YOUR IDEAS

There are many ways to start, many ways to order your thoughts. Some writers will think about an idea for a while, play around with it before writing it down. But it's important to get it down on paper in order to look at what you have, and to begin deciding where to go from here. It's also important because getting it down means transferring certain ideas out of your mind so that there's room for more to emerge. Good ideas evoke new ideas. Ideas connect with ideas, and—eureka!—the story begins to take form.

A script could be divided into five major components: the storylines, the characters, the underlying idea, the images, and the dialogue.

Each of these elements begin to take form at different times in the process. Some writers are particularly good at character and may begin with a character they've imagined. They let the story emerge from getting to know the character's decisions and actions.

Other writers begin with a story. They're intrigued with sequences of events. They like action, people doing exciting things.

5

And other writers might begin with an idea, something they want to explore. Perhaps it's "what happened to me one summer that changed me forever" or questions of justice, identity, about what happens to people who get sucked in by greed or corruption.

No matter where you start, at some point, all these elements need to come together in the script. And since they're all related, you can't work on character without story ideas emerging, or vice versa.

So you're looking for a method to bring together ideas while still letting them be fluid enough that you don't set your ideas in stone too quickly. You want plenty of opportunity for ideas to emerge, change, take new shapes.

To do this, some writers begin writing their ideas down on index cards.

THE INDEX CARD APPROACH

Since the storyline will rarely come to a writer full-blown, it's necessary to find some method to get down all the snippets of ideas that will all add up to make the script. Many writers use index cards, or writing their ideas in a loose leaf binder, to help them get started. Index cards are colorful, chaotic, and fluid—all of which is conducive to the beginning of the creative process.

Many writers who use index cards begin by buying index cards in many different colors. As they order their thoughts, each color represents different elements in the script. Perhaps you're writing a mystery and the white cards are used for all the scenes about the investigation. You use the pink cards for all the scenes about the love relationship between the detective and the blind witness. Yellow cards might contain notes on characters—including biography, character relationships, descriptions, and unusual habits. Blue cards might be notes on images—the immensity of the city (as in *The Fugitive*), or the gritty streets of New York (*Taxi Driver*). The notes on any one card might be short ("Upset, she calls the police"), or they be more extensive, describing the mood of the scene and some of the action. You might have separate cards that give research information—what happens at a crime scene? Where might a detective find finger-prints? What is gunshot residue and where do you find it?

Since the creative process wants to move from chaos to order, your mind will naturally begin to see the relationships of one card to another. You might find that your note about the love scene matches with your note about your character's desperate passion, which seems to fit well with your card that describes an image of an apartment made up of tight, broken-up spaces in the meat-packing area of the city (*Fatal Attraction*).

You might decide that your love scene would work well after the scene when your main character has taken her first air-plane flight, so you re-order your index cards to show that re-lationship (*Out of Africa*).

Using index cards is probably the most fluid approach to gathering ideas. It allows your ideas to emerge and to naturally find connections with other ideas. With index cards, you don't need to force the process by writing the script before you're ready. You aren't forcing yourself to make up a part of the story that isn't yet clear to you. Index cards allow for a great deal of shuffling around ideas from act to act or scene to scene. Ideas can be grouped together in a hundred different ways—although one way will eventually "feel more right" than the other ways.

Many writers put their index cards on a bulletin board, moving them around from act to act, and studying them daily for new possibilities. Some put their index card information on their computer. The danger, of course, is having nothing but a lot of different fragments of ideas with no order. But even though that might happen at first, eventually your mind will find a natu-ral connection between ideas. And the script notes will emerge organically, in a natural, creative, exciting, discovery.

Of course you don't know how many index cards you'll

need before the story, characters, theme, and images take shape. You may have 50, you may have 2000. But at some point the story will start asking you to write it down. Then you may want to move to writing an outline.

THE OUTLINE

The outline is simply a few lines about each of the scenes that make up the story. You may write them down on a few pieces of paper, on your computer, or in a loose-leaf binder with a page for each scene. A complete outline might consist of 50 or 100 lines, although you may not find it necessary to write out all the key scenes before beginning your script.

If you were to outline the beginning of *The African Queen*, it might look like this:

1. The Mission. Establish Rose and her brother at the mission. Allnutt arrives.

2. Scene to establish the relationship of Allnutt to Rose and brother.

3. Germans come—kill brother and natives, destroy village.

4. Allnutt returns. Bury brother. He and Rose plan their escape.
Etc.

With just this much information, it's possible to begin writing the script, although some writers might choose to first expand on each scene with more character and story information. Or, they might first write up the storyline in treatment form.

THE TREATMENT

Some writers begin with a treatment, which is basically a narration or synopsis of your story. Like a short story, it's fairly brief—usually about eight to fifteen pages—and it tells the beginning, middle, and end of you're story. If your story has come to you fairly full-blown, the treatment is an opportunity to write down the narration in logical order. By looking at the narrative line, you'll be able to see if the story makes sense, adds up, has movement and direction. If one event doesn't seem to relate to another event, you may have gone off on some tangent that has nothing to do with the story. If your story is bogged down, you'll see exactly where action is missing. If the climax isn't clear, you'll be able to see that your story doesn't build or has lost direction toward the end.

If you're writing a treatment for a studio or production company, they'll usually ask for five to twelve pages. But a treatment can also be used as a creative tool. Some writers use the treatment as a form of stream-of-consciousness writing—letting all the ideas come out. They might write for five pages about the feeling of her apartment or about why these people are attracted to each other, and then sum up the next eight scenes with a line or two. The treatment can get the initial spark down on paper. It can be an opportunity to let all the ideas come popping out, to start getting the flow of dialogue, to begin feeling out the style of the story.

Treatments can help you formulate your story by seeing the problems and continually reworking the story. However, particularly in the beginning stages, it's important to keep the treatment a fluid document that can change and grow in the rewriting. For some writers, once it's written down, it's the truth. There's something pretty about a neat and cleanly written storyline, even if it's not yet worked out. If this is the case for you, write on the back of scratch paper so that you can play around with ideas, go out on a limb, insert a crazy story idea that you may need to toss out later. It can free you up to continue to make changes in your storyline until you feel it's "right"—clear, interesting, and well-structured.

KEEPING A JOURNAL

While treatments can be a good method for getting a clear sense of your story, they are sometimes less helpful for character and thematic development. That's why some writers work with journals before writing the script. The journal gives the writer the opportunity to explore the characters and themes in the same way they might explore their own lives and issues.

The journal approach affords opportunity to get more deeply inside your characters—to find what they think, how they feel, what bothers them, what they care about, how they react. Just as you might keep a journal about your inner thoughts, you may find that the journal approach takes you inside the character in order to help you find the character's body and voice.

The journal might be written in first person, as though you are the character writing his or her thoughts and experiences, or written as a third-person account, as though the characters are your friends or someone you're observing. It might contain character descriptions and actions as well as associations. You might answer questions: How much money does the character earn? What's his family like? What kind of school did she go to?

You might create a character by writing about people you know and how the character is like them. Maybe you begin to think of character traits that interest you, or why a character does what she does. Maybe you write about your feelings about the woman who left you five years ago and base a story on that experience. Or maybe you remember a summer romance and write down all the details that give that story a new twist. And as you work through your ideas, something begins to spark inside of you. You get more excited, ideas come. Maybe you use them. Maybe they take you somewhere else.

Themes can also be explored through a journal. Scripts contain ideas, and ideas need to be worked through as much as the story and characters. If your theme is about the Negative, Spreading Influence of Violence (*Unforgiven*), you might make journal entries about the various ways and the various levels that violence affects the different characters. You might discuss the bad dreams your character has when he encounters violence. You might explore the universal attraction to violence that seems to exist in all people. You might discuss the bonding that happens through violence (perhaps discussing war-time bonding or the bonding through gangs) in order to make sure that your theme speaks to a contemporary audience.

Whereas the treatment might help you check your story, the journal can help you get inside your characters or your theme.

At this point, you may have tried out several of these tools and you find that your characters have begun to talk to you. If so, you might want to get out your tape recorder and try another technique.

TALKING TO YOURSELF WITH THE TAPE RECORDER

Every day of your life you talk. You're used to it. Talking to a tape recorder can be very freeing, giving you a tool to let ideas flow in an uninhibited way. Perhaps you are beginning to think of chunks of dialogue for your characters. The voices are coming at you. They're talking so fast that you can barely get them down on paper. Perhaps you're driving in your car. Or stuck in traffic. Or you wake up in the middle of the night with a thought, a piece of dialogue. Suddenly you hear those words. If something is working well, no matter what your situation, you want to get it down while it's hot. The tape recorder gives you the opportunity to catch words and ideas whenever they come— as well as to hear them spoken, rather than see them written.

Any number of ideas might come to you. You might play around with dialogue to express attitudes, or to help you think through ways to express the issues in the script, or to explore character relationships. Maybe the dialogue comes full-blown, or you keep a few key words or a turn of phrase while reworking everything else.

Of course, there is a disadvantage of tape recorders. You need to transcribe what you said. But you don't need to transcribe everything. If you like what comes to you, transcribe it. If not, don't delete it. Later, you may want to go back to the tape to re-capture the inspiration for the dialogue, or the relationship of one idea to another. Although you may not use it, it may be important to remember why the words came out in that particular order.

You may decide that instead of doing all these techniques, you just want to get to work writing. And there are writers who will take that approach.

GETTING IT DOWN

Some ideas come to writers full-blown. They see the movie in their head. If that's the case with you, start writing the script immediately. At some point you may get stuck, and need to return to one of these techniques, but there are writers who simple sit down and write the script.

Or you may be a first-time scriptwriter. You're ready to write your first script, but writing 120 pages seems overwhelming. In that case, if you have a storyline, you may want to start by simply getting the story down in script form, without preparation, and then reworking it. Until you find your creative process, there are fears. Can I actually write 120 pages? Is this going to be worth my time? How long will it take? Getting 120 pages down on paper, no matter how good or bad they are, gets rid of the "I wonder if I can do it?" problems. Rarely will this draft be workable, because there is little craft in this process. But there may be some artistic, magical scenes or dialogue. You may need to start all over again from the beginning, preparing and crafting the story. But the knowledge that you've done it once makes the next time easier.

Most experienced writers, however, work out their stories and characters very carefully before starting to write the script. The more time spent beforehand on planning the script, the faster the script gets written. However, you might decide to apply part of this technique by doing all of the previous methods of preparation, but then, once you begin writing, keep writing. Some writers, once they start writing, don't go back until they've finished the script. They recognize that once the script starts flowing, it's not a good idea to interrupt the process to change grammar, fix typos, play around with several approaches to a scene. They want to just get everything down.

COMPUTER PROGRAMS

We live in the Information Age. Most writers write on a computer. Many use the Internet and communicate with other writers through an Electronic Bulletin Board. It's only natural that a variety of screenplay computer-software programs are now on the market to help a writer write, and rewrite, the script.

Here, I'm not talking about programs for formatting your script (such as *Scriptor, MovieMaster,* and *Scriptwrite*), but programs designed to help you organize and prepare to write your script. (The current ones on the market include *Collaborator, Storyline,* and *Dramatica*). For some, these programs are controversial. It looks as if they are applying a paint-by-number approach to writing a script, telling the writer where to place every event and assuring the writer that if they follow everything in the system, they'll have a "perfect" script.

Other writers see these programs as a catalyst for their creativity. They're a guide to keep them on track, a help to knowing what to do next.

What does a screenplay program do? When can it work for you? What do you need to beware of?

At the very least, a screenplay program helps you organize your thoughts and put all your information together in one place. Instead of index cards, which you will need to write and rewrite, or scratch pads with copious notes, all the information on story and character and premise and theme all are in one place, to be worked and reworked as new ideas emerge.

A screenplay program helps you be aware of the issues that you need to address as you write the script. There are hundreds, if not thousands, of elements that make a script work. Experienced writers know many of these elements subconsciously, but the new writer doesn't yet have as many tools. The screenplay program keeps reminding the writer: Have you clearly worked out your character's biography? Do you understand what your characters want and what action are they going to take to get it? What's the conflict? What are the problems your character needs to solve? Who's the audience? Do your character's choices make sense? What are the character traits of your main characters and supporting characters?

Some of the questions are not all that different than the questions you'll find at the end of each of the chapters of this book. Like these questions, they are designed to keep the writer cognizant of the issues that need to be resolved to make the script work.

A good screenplay program works as a partner, or collaborator, to keep moving you forward in your thinking. Most of them will contain definitions, information, analysis of great scripts, and how these various elements work within that script. So, they serve as a teaching tool as well as a writing tool.

Some of them have room for playing around with ideas. Most are designed to ask you questions at various points in your story creation. Many of them organize material so that you can see the relationship of elements within the script.

Remember that every system is based on the dramatic theory of the designer. You'll have to learn the designer's vocabulary. There may be a number of concepts to learn before you can even begin to write.

Implicit in a screenplay program is a certain logic. A computer program needs to be constructed rationally, even though your approach to each script may not be rational. Maybe you want to begin constructing your character from a piece of dialogue, or a sense of the character's energy and rhythm, or the color of a character's dress. But when you pull up the character questions, you see the same questions each time, which may make you think that there's only one way to go through the process of creating the script. The screenplay program can't take into account the hundreds of different starting places, or the thousands of different processes that can get you to a good script.

Ultimately, the test of any method is whether it's an effective tool for you. Any system is only as good as the artistry of the writer using it. If a writer simply fills in the blanks, the writer may create a so-called workable script, but it will probably be predictable and derivative. If the method doesn't help you shape and structure the story, or create exciting and imaginative characters, then it's not the system for you. A good system should give flexibility and room for your own creative process. It should work as a creative collaborator with you, helping you understand the issues as well as shape your script.

THERE'S NO ONE RIGHT WAY

Many writers will turn to different methods for different scripts. Part of the art of writing includes having many different tools and using different tools to get you into your script in different ways. If one doesn't work, hopefully another does. But remember, the object of these techniques is for them to serve the actual writing of the script. Some writers have hundreds of ideas, thousands of index cards, but no script. At some point, it needs to be written down, it needs to find its shape.

The creation of the script will need not only your knowledge and craft, but will need your art—your particular voice, your vision, your perspective, your experience, your unique attitudes. All methods and all concepts, while helping you craft your story, hopefully will also be a catalyst to help you become a better artist.

A large part of the work of writing a script is accomplished with all this preparation. When you've attended to your preliminary work, when you've done your preparation well, the actual writing of the script will be much easier.

For most, writing a script, from the idea through the first draft, takes about three to six months, although some writers may take a year or more. I know of some writers who have written a script in two or three weeks. Other writers might take five years. Rewrites might take an additional two weeks—or two years. There is no correct time limit that you must follow to create your script. There is no right or wrong way of writing a script. There is no one creative process.

APPLICATION

There is a reason why you're writing a script. There are questions you can ask to help you be in touch with your passion, your creativity, and the method that can best help you prepare your thoughts before writing the script.

Before beginning to write the script, ask yourself:

What's the one thing that makes me want to write this story?

Have I thought through all the elements of my script—the story, the theme, the characters, the images, and have I begun to think of dialogue?

Do I hear the voices of my characters? Are they beginning to talk to me so that when I start to write the dialogue, I'll have real characters talking?

Have I taken enough time to explore the story and characters without rushing ahead to write the script?

Have I superimposed rules onto my story and characters, or have I tried to allow them to grow organically?

Am I focusing on my passion, my art, on what I really want to say? Or am I being overly concerned about marketing the script, how commercial it is, how much money I'm going to make, and how famous I'll become? Am I planning my Oscar-acceptance speech before it's written, or am I willing to wait for the nomination?

Have I remembered to keep my eye on the process rather than trying to find fast results?

Once you've gone through this preparation, you'll be ready to begin writing the script. When you reach that point, you're ready to structure and shape your story into a dramatic form. You're ready to begin shaping your beginning, your middle, and your end.

Chapter Two

The Three-Act Structure: Why You Need It and What to Do with It

You're a writer. You've just finished 115 pages of a terrific script. It's good, you know it's good. You've shown it to several friends who tell you it's better than *E.T.* But you have a gnawing feeling that something isn't quite right. Someplace, maybe in the second act, it seems like all the elements don't fit. It doesn't add up. It doesn't feel as good as it can be. You begin to doubt.

Or you're a producer who wants desperately to option a specific script. It's unique, it's funny, it would make a great vehicle for one of the hottest actors in town. But the script isn't working. It seems inconsistent, the ending is much better than the beginning, and there seem to be too many characters. You don't want to let the deal go, but you can't commit to an unworkable story.

Or you're a development executive, three weeks away from shooting. The script is still coming in at 138 pages, the second act is lagging, and the star doesn't like the way her character develops in Act Two.

All of these are normal situations that must be confronted in order to make the script work. They're all basically structural problems. It's not that the story isn't good. The problem lies with the construction of the story. The script doesn't yet work—but where to start?

THE THREE-ACT STRUCTURE

Writing and rewriting is a process that demands both an overview and great attention to detail. Like a script, the process has a beginning, a middle, and, thankfully, an end.

Part of writing and rewriting a good script includes finding a strong structure that will support your story. It means constructing your story in a way that will give it form, focus, momentum, and clarity. It means finding ways to help your audience "get with" your story and involving your audience all along the way. It means crafting your story into dramatic form.

Dramatic composition, almost from the beginning of drama, has tended toward the three-act structure. Whether it's a Greek tragedy, a five-act Shakespearean play, a four-act dramatic series, or a seven-act Movie-of-the-Week, we still see the basic three-act structure: beginning, middle, and end—or **set-up, development,** and **resolution.**

In most three-act plays, the three-act structure is very clear —the curtain goes down at the end of Act One, showing the end of the set-up of the story, and at the end of Act Two, showing the end of story development. Then Act Three proceeds, building toward the climax and resolution.

Television artificially stops the show for commercials, creating a two-act structure (for sitcoms), seven acts (for a two-hour television movie), or four acts (for a dramatic series). But in a good television show, the three-act structure is still contained within these more artificial act endings. There is still a clear set-up, development, and resolution.

Although there are no stopping places in feature films, the act structure is still there—helping to move and focus the story. As a result of these similarities in all dramatic forms, all the comments I make about feature-film structure are equally relevant to television and theatre.

These acts for a feature film usually include a ten- to fifteen-page set-up of the story, about twenty pages of development in Act One, a long second act that might run forty five to sixty pages, and a fairly fast-paced third act of twenty to thirty-five pages. Each act has a different focus. The movement out of one act and into the next is usually accomplished by an action or an event called a **turning point.** If we were to graph the three-act structure, it would look something like this:

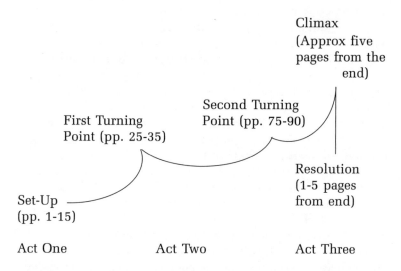

Climax
(Approx five
pages from the
end)

Second Turning
Point (pp. 75-90)

First Turning
Point (pp. 25-35)

Resolution
(1-5 pages
from end)

Set-Up
(pp. 1-15)

Act One   Act Two   Act Three

Each section of this structure has a different purpose. The set-up accomplishes different goals from the second turning point. The development of Act One is different from the development of Act Two. The pacing of Act Three is usually faster than that of the other two acts.

Reworking the script is more manageable after identifying and focusing on the set-up, the turning points, and the resolution.

The Set-Up

The first few minutes of a story can be the most important. Many scripts have problems with the set-up. It's unclear, it's unfocused. Or it sets up everything but the story.

The purpose of the set-up is to tell us all the vital information we need to get the story started. Who are the main characters? What's the story about? Where is it located? Is it a comedy or drama, farce or tragedy?

The set-up is designed to give us a clue about the **spine** or **direction** of the story. It begins to focus the situation into a coherent storyline. It gives movement to the story. It also helps orient the audience so that they can enjoy the show without asking such questions as "What's it about?" "What are they doing?" "Why are they doing it?"

Begin with an Image   In most good films, the set-up begins with an **image**. We see a visualization that gives us a strong sense of the place, mood, texture, and sometimes the theme. This first image could be a space battle (*Star Wars*), street gangs in New York (*West Side Story*), a woman singing in the mountains (*The Sound of Music*), or statues of lions that ominously guard a haunted library (*Ghostbusters*).

Films that begin with dialogue, rather than a particular visual image, tend to be more difficult to understand. This is because the eye is quicker at grasping details than the ear. If important information is given verbally, before the audience has adjusted to the style, the place, and the sounds, it's difficult to remember the words. As a result, we may not know how to incorporate them into the story.

So begin with an image, a feeling, a sense of where we are, a sense of pacing, a sense of the style of the film. Tell us as much as you can with this image. Get us into the mood of the piece. If possible, create a metaphor for the film, telling us something about the theme through the pictures you create.

Some of the most popular films have created vibrant and

memorable images. Let's look at two of them: *Witness,* and *The African Queen.*

The first three minutes of *Witness* are almost completely image-oriented. With music in the background, we see:

Grain blowing in the wind.

Amish dressed in traditional black, walking through the grain.

Amish wagons moving to the clip-clop of horses.

A farmhouse.

A funeral.

Faces.

And the first words we hear are in Dutch-German.

We might ask, after seeing the first few minutes of *Witness,* "What does it tell us? What have we learned from what we've seen?"

Witness begins with a particular rhythm and a slow, lyrical pacing. These first few moments of *Witness* show us a gentle folk, a community, a sense of participation and support. They're a people who live close to the land, as evidenced by the grain images. Their life is slower than city life. We have a sense that these people have close connections with the earth, and with each other.

With these first few minutes of the film, the **theme** has begun—the theme of community. As the story proceeds, we'll see this community image build and contrast with the faster-paced, more violent world of the police.

Notice also that there is no dialogue here. The image builds and builds, detail by detail, until we have a sense of the location, the pacing, the mood, and the texture.

The African Queen begins with a sense of context and texture, as it describes "A Native Village in a clearing between the jungle and the river. Late morning."

LONG SHOT—A CHAPEL

Intense light and heat, a stifling silence. Then the SOUND of a reedy organ, of two voices that make the words distinct, and of the miscellaneous, shy, muffled, dragging voices, beginning a hymn:

VOICES

(singing)
"Guide me O Thou Great Jehovah . . ."

INT.—CHAPEL—THE LENGTH OF THE BLEAK CHAPEL PAST THE CONGREGATION, ON BROTHER AT THE LECTERN, AND ROSE, AT THE ORGAN.

BROTHER

"Pilgrim through this barren land . . ."

Brother is middle-aged, rock-featured, bald, sweating painfully, very much in earnest. He is very watchful of his flock. He sings as loud as he can, rather nasally, and tries to drive the meaning of each word home as if it were a nail. He is beating with his hand and trying hard to whip up the dragging tempo:

BROTHER

"I am weak, but Thou art mighty . . ."

ROSE, early thirties, tight-featured and tight-haired . . . She is pumping the pedals vigorously, spreading with her knees the wings of wood that control the loudness, utilizing various stops for expressiveness of special phrases, and rather desperately studying the open hymnal, just managing to play the right notes—a very busy woman. She too, is singing her best and loudest . . .

ROSE
"Hold me with Thy powerful hand."

(Into this most passionately pious moment, comes)

A fiery, cloudy pillar, a queer SOUND, steadily louder: the
absurdly flatulent, yammering syncopation of a rachitic
steam motor. Eyes begin to wander from hymnals: CUT IN
Brother frowning and singing harder trying to impose order;
attention to the hymn begins to fall apart a little:

LONG SHOT—THE AFRICAN QUEEN
whose whistle lets out a steamy whinny, then REPEATS
it, with great self-satisfaction. She is squat, flat-bottomed,
thirty feet long. A tattered awning roofs in six feet of her
stern. Amidship stands her boiler and engine. A stumpy
funnel reaches up a little higher than the awning.

ON SECOND WHINNY   CUT TO:

MEDIUM CLOSE SHOT—ALLNUTT—ON HIS BOAT
He is in worn, rather befouled white clothes. He is bare-
footed and his feet are cocked up and he is sitting on his
shoulder blades, smoking a bad cigar. He wears a ratty
boater, slantwise against the sunlight. He is attended by two
young negroes, so tall, thin and gracile, they suggest black
macaroni. One is proudly and busily puttering at the engine, which requires a lot of attention: the other is fanning
ALLNUTT, who is feeling just fine . . . The Queen begins
to swerve toward shore.

The image continues with the commotion of frustration,
as Brother and Rose try, with great ardor, to bring the hymn to
a dignified close, and Allnutt comes closer, smoking a cigar and
bringing the mail.

This first image is rich with contrasts. Within minutes we are introduced to the "heathen blacks" and the "christianized natives." We are also introduced to the pious white missionaries, and the equally unpious Allnutt, to the uptight Rose and the loose Allnutt, to the singers and the nonsingers, and to the "civilized" white man and woman, trying to impose order on the "primitive." Into this world comes a wisp of smoke and the sound of a whistle, which will connect this far-off place with the problems of a world war.

Finding the Catalyst   After the initial image begins the story, we need to be introduced to any important characters who will be part of the plot. We need information about the situation: "Where are we? What's going on here?" And something, some event, needs to start the story. I call this particular event the **catalyst.**

The catalyst begins the action of the story. Something happens—an explosion, a murder, a letter arrives, perhaps Aunt Mary appears on the doorstep—and from that moment on the story is defined. We now know what the story is about—what the spine of the story will be.

The catalyst is the first main "push" that gets the plot moving. Something happens, or someone makes a decision. The main character is set in motion. The story has begun.

There are three different kinds of catalysts. The strongest are specific actions that begin a story. In *Witness,* a murder happens and John Book is called in to solve it. A ghost is seen in the library in *Ghostbusters.* And a swimmer is killed by a shark in *Jaws.*

Sometimes the catalyst is a piece of information that a character receives, orienting us to the subject of the story. This is true in many Movies-of-the-Week, which often deal with issues, crimes, and diseases. A woman is told that she has cancer, a man is promoted to a new job, a couple is told that they will never have children.

Sometimes a catalyst is situational, a series of incidents that add up over a period of time to orient us. In *Back to the Fu-*

ture, we don't know about the time machine until twenty-two minutes into the film. But we do know that a crazy inventor is one of the main characters. We also know that Marty is supposed to meet him at 1:15 a.m. at Twin Pines Mall, and that the meeting is important—and secretive. As the situation builds, we become more and more curious. Eventually, by the end of Act One, the spine of the story becomes clear.

Tootsie also has a situational beginning. We know that Michael is an out-of-work actor. We know that he's difficult to work with. We know that he's a good actor. We know that no one will hire him because of his attitude. And we know that there is a job available on a soap opera—for a woman. It takes almost the entire first act to build this information, but by the end of Act One we're oriented, and the story is ready to unfold.

Raise the Central Question   The set-up, however, is still not complete. The image may have oriented us, and the cata-lyst has begun the story, but there's one more ingredient nec-essary before we're ready to begin the story.

Every story, in a sense, is a mystery. It asks a question in the set-up that will be answered at the climax. Usually a prob-lem is introduced, or a situation that needs to be resolved is presented. This situation or problem raises a question in our minds, such as "Will John Book get the murderer?" (*Witness*); "Will the Germans get away with their massacre?" (*The African Queen*); "Will Martin catch the shark?" (*Jaws*).

Onced it is raised, everything that happens in the story re-lates to that question. Most often, the **central question** is an-swered "yes" in the **climax** of the story. "Will John Book get the murderer?" Yes. "Will Allnutt and Rose blow up the *Louisa*?" Yes. "Will Martin catch the shark?" Yes. But we don't learn the answers until the end, and although we might guess the end-ing, we remain interested in what will happen along the way.

Once the central question has been asked, the set-up is complete. The story is now ready to unfold.

Setting Act One Action

By the end of the Set-Up, we are probably about ten to fifteen minutes into the film. It's important to keep the Set-Up tight because the audience will become impatient if they don't have some sense of the story after fifteen minutes. There are, of course, a number of foreign films and some American films that make the audience wait much longer for a sense of the story spine. But the longer the story waits to get started, the more danger there is that there might not be a story spine at all, or that the audience won't find it. And although some of these may be artisitic, rarely are they box-office successes. Since I believe that you can have both artisitic and well-crafted scripts, without compromise, I recommend a tight, clean, clear beginning.

This set-up will then be followed by the Act One Development. After the set-up, more information is necessary to orient us to the story. We need to learn more about the characters. We need to see the characters in action before we see the characters develop in Act Two. We might need to know more about the **backstory**, or the **situation.** Where is the character coming from? What's motivating the character? What's the central conflict? Who's the antagonist?

To analyze Act One, we need to understand the important **beats** that prepare us for the unfolding of the story.

We might think of a beat as a single dramatic moment or a single dramatic event. In music, single beats together make up a measure. If you add more beats, you create a phrase, and then a melody, and finally an entire song. In drama, it works the same way. Single dramatic beats or moments, placed together, create a scene. And the beats in a scene, together, create the beats of an act, and the beats of each act, together, create a story.

In *Witness*, there are a number of necessary beats that define the central action of Act One—trying to identify the murderer:

John Book shows Samuel a suspect for identification.

John arranges for Rachel and Samuel to stay another day.

John shows Samuel a line-up.

John shows Samuel mug shots.

Samuel sees the photo of McFee and identifies him as the murderer.

John Book tells Police Chief Paul Schaeffer.

McFee tries to kill John, and John realizes that Paul is in on the murder.

These beats are not the main focus of the story. They are not what the story is about. But they do prepare us for what is to come next.

Why Turning Points?

A good story always remains interesting. It retains interest because of the unpredictable and intriguing twists and turns in the action along the way to the climax. If the story were completely linear and developed totally from the first push of the catalyst to the climax, our interest would lag and the focus would be unclear.

Although twists and turns can happen throughout a story, in the three-act structure there are two turning points that need to happen to keep the action moving—one at the beginning of Act Two and one at the beginning of Act Three. These help a story change direction. New events unfold. New decisions are made. As a result of these two turning points, the story achieves momentum and retains its focus.

Generally, the first turning point happens about a half-hour into the film, with the second one coming about twenty to thirty minutes before the end of the film. Each of these turning points accomplishes a variety of functions:

It turns the action around in a new direction.

It raises the central question again, and makes us wonder about the answer.

It's often a moment of decision or commitment on the part of the main character.

It raises the stakes.

It pushes the story into the next act.

It takes us into a new arena and gives us a sense of a different focus for the action.

A strong turning point will accomplish all of these functions, although many turning points accomplish only some of them.

Witness is one of the best examples of a tightly structured script—and the turning points are some of the strongest you can find. The first turning point occurs about thirty-two minutes into the story, just after John Book finishes explaining to the police, Chief Paul Schaeffer, that the boy has given positive identification on McFee.

Schaeffer asks, "Who else knows about this?" Book replies, "Just us." Schaeffer suggests that they keep it that way. John Book then returns home, only to be ambushed in his garage by McFee. As he realizes he's been shot, he remembers Schaeffer's words, "Who else knows about this?" And his answer, "Just us."

Notice what this accomplishes. Up to this point, John has been pursuing the normal channels for trying to find a murderer. He's checked the line-up, he's looked through the book, and it now seems as if his work is ended. Paul has said that he will take care of everything. The action has almost come to a halt.

But with this turning point, suddenly everything is different. A strong action takes place—McFee tries to kill John Book. And with this action, John realizes that Paul is in on the crime. At this point, we wonder again, "Will John get the murderer?" Before, it looked as if the answer was "yes." Now the answer seems to be "maybe not."

The stakes are now higher. John must leave, he must escape. His life is now in danger for the first time, along with the lives of Rachel and Samuel. At this moment, John makes some decisions—to destroy the files, take Rachel and Samuel back to the farm, and escape until the situation cools off.

In *Witness*, we see examples of a turning point that contains two different beats. The first happens when John is shot and he realizes that Paul is a murderer. This turns the action around and takes us out of Act One. But we need another beat to move us into Act Two. At this point, we only know that John plans to escape, but the Act Two action of staying at the Amish Farm has not yet begun. That happens when John blacks out from his wound, drives his car into the bird house, and needs to be hidden at the Lapp farm. A moment before, John's intention was to drive away, and the Act Two action might have been about a man hiding out in a seedy hotel. Now, John is forced to stay at the Amish farm, and the second act will revolve around what happens as a result.

In *Tootsie*, Act One builds up details about Michael, his ability as an actor and acting teacher, his difficult personality, his search for work. But with the first turning point, about twenty-two minutes into the film, Michael has become Dorothy. Now Act Two is ready to progress, as the film explores all the twists, turns, complexities, and insights when a man becomes a woman.

In *The African Queen,* about half an hour into the story, after Allnutt and Rose have left for who-knows-where, Rose gets the idea to torpedo the German Ship *Louisa*, and finally Allnut agrees. This decision leads into Act Two, which will be about the journey.

The Second Turning Point

After about an hour of developing Act Two, there's another turning point—the second turning point—which also changes the action around, moving the story into Act Three. It accomplishes the same things as the first turning point:

It turns the action around in a new direction.

It raises the central question again and makes us wonder about the answer.

It's often a moment of decision or commitment on the part of the main character.

It raises the stakes.

It pushes the story into the next act.

It takes us into a new arena and gives us a sense of a different focus for the action.

But the second turning point does one thing more: It speeds up the action. It makes the third act more intense than the other two. It gives a sense of urgency, or momentum, to the story. It pushes the story toward its conclusion.

Sometimes, a second turning point is a "ticking clock"— "Well, James Bond, you have six hours or I blow up Paris!" Or: "If you don't do what I ask in twenty-four hours, I'll report you to the police." Or: "At noon, they'll come looking for you!"

Sometimes, the second turning point comes in two beats. These beats are often a *dark moment*, followed by a *new* stimulus.

In a mystery, this dark moment might happen when the detective has almost given up—the case seems unsolvable. Suddenly, the detective sees the solution, and the third act proceeds as he finds the villian. Or in a horror film, the dark moment comes when the scientist realizes that he'll never be able to destroy the monster. And, a few moments later, a new plan is hatched.

In *Cocoon*, we see an excellent example of a two-part turning point. After the people from the retirement home have drained the energy from the pool, Walter sees the Anterian in the cocoon die. This death is a dark moment for Walter—it puts his mission in jeopardy and raises the stakes. All seems lost. His mission has failed. But a new stimulus comes into the action five minutes later. Grandpa volunteers the retired people to help put the cocoons back in the water to save them for a future trip. A new stimulus—a new solution—is found to solve the problem and lead us into Act Three.

In *Witness*, the second turning point happens when John is discovered and Paul and McFee now know where he's hiding. This discovery happens in several beats:

> John hears that his partner is dead and tells Paul that he's coming after him.

> When several punks try to pick a fight with the Amish, John obliges.

> A policeman goes around the corner and realizes that this is the man mentioned by Paul. Off-screen, he tells Paul that John is staying with Eli Lapp.

The second turning point happens the moment that John punches out the punk. This, together with the police identifying John Book, turns the action around, leading to the final shoot-out in Act Three.

The Big Finish

The **climax** usually happens about one to five pages from the end of the script, followed by a short **resolution** that ties up all loose ends. The climax is the end of the story: It's the *big finish*. It's the moment when the problem is resolved, the question is answered, the tension lets up, and we know that everything is all right.

> John captures Paul and we know that there's nothing left to do but say good-bye.

> Marty gets "back to the future."

> Tootsie is unmasked and he gets the girl.

The Ghostbusters get the big one, as do Martin and Matt in *Jaws*.

Once the climax has been reached, the party is over and it's time to go home. There's nothing more to be said, and it's a good idea not to say it. Although the temptation might be to prolong the story, to add another piece of information, or one more image, it's over and it's time to write "The End."

In addition to crafting the three acts of a story, there are other ways to add structure to a script. Two of these methods include using the credit sequence and the midpoint scene to further shape the script.

THE CREDIT SEQUENCE

A movie can begin in three different ways. It can begin with several minutes of credits, and then the story begins. These credits can be as simple as white print on a black screen, or vice versa (see most of Woody Allen's films), or very classy written credits (see most films before the 1950s and such films as *Room With a View* or *Age of Innocence*.)

Or the credits might occur over images and action, usually without dialogue (as in *The Silence of the Lambs, Jaws, Fatal Attraction*), so the filmmaker is setting up a great deal of context and information underneath the credits, even though the story has not yet begun.

Since the 1980s, there has been another approach to credits—an increasing number of films have a pre-credit sequence. In most cases, there are about two to three minutes of a montage, or one or two short scenes that set up characters, or a scene or two that sets up a context or a situation. These initial scenes are then followed by either written credits (see *City Slickers*) or credits over action (*WarGames*).

This use of the pre-credit sequence can give further shape to a story because it allows the writer to approach the story in two different ways, usually by first establishing the situation, then by introducing the main characters. For instance, in *Ghostbusters,* the pre-credit sequence introduces the library ghost. Then credits begin, and after the credits, the main characters are introduced. Or, in *Broadcast News,* first the characters are introduced as children, then the credits begin and the story begins with them as grown-up broadcast journalists.

In most cases, these pre-credit sequences are short, usually about two-three minutes, but occasionally there are very long sequences. There is a seven minute pre-credit sequence at the beginning of *WarGames.* The beginning of *Born on the Fourth of July* is also about seven minutes long. In both cases, the pre-credit sequence set up the context, but the story doesn't really begin until after the credits.

Although almost all executives, producers and directors will tell a writer that the credits really are not their business (and in most cases, there is no reason for a writer to write anything about the credits), there are times when the credits are part of the shape of the film. It then becomes necessary for the writer to communicate this structure to the reader and the producers.

The use of credits have become very creative over the last few years. For an example of a particularly interesting credit sequence watch the credits of *The Fugitive,* interspersed within the first eleven minutes of the film. They begin over the slow motion, black-and-white murder. They then are interspersed through the arrest and questioning of Richard Kimble. They stop for a few minutes and then begin again after Kimble is sentenced and continue as the bus leaves to transport him to prison. Here, they help move and shape the set-up of the film, dividing the beginning into several sections and adding to the fast pace of the film.

THE MID POINT SCENE

The midpoint scene occurs just where you'd expect it to be—about half way through the script. Syd Field, in *The Screenwriter's Workbook*, says that it divides the story in half, introducing an event or line of dialogue that helps structure Act Two.

In my work consulting on more than 1500 scripts, and teaching many of the best films, I don't find midpoint scenes in every film, but when I do find them, they are excellent structural tools to help structure the difficult second act.

Besides dividing the entire script in half, the midpoint scene divides the second act in half, creating a direction for the first half of Act Two, and giving a change in direction for the second half of the act, while still keeping the overall focus of Act Two which has been determined by the first turning point.

Some of the best midpoint scenes can be found in mysteries and thrillers. In *Fatal Attraction*, Alex announces that she's pregnant halfway through the film. The entire second act is about "disengaging from Alex," but the midpoint scene pulls Dan back into her life, although unwittingly.

In *The Fugitive*, Richard Kimble gets computer information about the one-armed man halfway through the second act. Here the first half of the act is about getting away and getting to Chicago—it's basically chase scenes. The second half of Act Two consists of Richard investigating the one-armed man, and Sam Gerard investigating Richard. Although the film never loses sight of the fact that Gerard wants to find Richard, Richard's investigation gives additional structure to the act.

In *The Silence of the Lambs*, Hannibal Lecter is moved to Memphis at the midpoint scene, thereby changing the direction of the second half of Act Two. The midpoint of *Tootsie* shows Dorothy's fame increasing as she becomes the darling of audiences and media, appearing in national magazines.

Using the midpoint scene can be confusing for many writers. In my consulting work, I've discovered that many writers mistake the midpoint for the first turning point, thereby throwing the structure off and creating scripts where the second act doesn't begin until halfway through the script. However, if the writer begins by first creating a clear three-act structure, often a midpoint scene will naturally emerge. Then, in the rewriting process, the writer can further strengthen and focus the scene.

WHAT GOES WRONG WITH STRUCTURE?

Rarely will you see a film where each act is equally well structured. Not everyone in Hollywood knows how to structure a script, nor is every brilliant writer necessarily a brilliant structuralist. As a result, most films will have flaws in one of their acts.

Sometimes, you'll see a very slow set-up. For instance, the brilliant film *Tender Mercies* had a long and subtle set-up that demanded a great deal of patience while waiting for the story to get started. So, too, did *Kiss of a Spider Woman,* which focused on character and image at the beginning and played the first catalyst (when the William Hurt character agreed to gather information from his cellmate, a late set-up about twenty minutes into the film) off-screen. In a feature film, you'll usually sit it out, since rarely do people walk out of a film in the first twenty minutes. In a television show, however, a slow set-up is deadly and will usually lead to switching channels.

Some films wait too long for their first turning point, which leads to a lag in the action in Act One and condenses the development of Act Two, which can easily lose audience interest. This occurred in the film *Awakenings*, where the 1st turning point was late (at about forty-three minutes into the film) and the happier second act was condensed.

Some films place the second turning point too early, causing Act Three to lag, or place it too late, so that there isn't suffucient time to develop tension and suspense leading to the big finish.

Some films have a long resolution, which continues on and

on, even after the climax has been reached. *Passage to India* and *The Color Purple* were criticized for long resolutions of over twenty minutes. If the resolution is too long, the audience feels that there's not a clear ending, or that they've already seen the ending and wonder why the film isn't over yet.

Witness is one of the best films to study to learn about structure. It's clear, concise, and you can feel the movement from act to act, as well as see how the arena and action change.

Other well-structured films to study include: *Unforgiven, The Fugitive, Ruthless People, Back to the Future,* and *Tootsie.* Like many films, the turning points are not readily apparent in a first viewing. However, the test for these films, as with any film or script, is the same. If you feel focused throughout, without any lags in your interest or in the movement of the story, you can be fairly certain that the script is well-structured.

APPLICATION

Restructuring the story is much of the work of a rewrite. Rarely in the first draft are the three acts clear. Usually one act is stronger than the others. Sometimes a turning point is misplaced. Or a turning point might be weak, hindering the movement of the script from act to act.

As you look through the structure of your script, ask the following questions:

Have you begun with an image?

Does the image give a sense of the style and feeling of the story?

Do you have a clear catalyst to begin the story? Is it strong and dramatic, preferably expressed through action?

Does your central question set up the climax of your story? Is the central question clear? Does each turning point bring up the central question again?

Do you have a clear first turning point? Does it lead into the action of Act Two? Is your second turning point clear? Does it set up the climax.

Is your climax a big finish? Is your resolution quick?

Now you've reworked your major plot line. It's consistent. It's dramatic. It moves. But rarely will you have only one plot line. Integrating the subplots is the next important step.

Chapter Three

What Do Subplots Do?

A workable subplot performs several functions. The overall function of a subplot is to add dimension to the script. When the protagonist is doing the story, he or she is busy with action. But the subplots give the protagonist an opportunity to smell the flowers, to fall in love, to enjoy a hobby, to learn a new skill.

A good subplot pushes the plot line, often changing the direction of the plot line because of the effect of the subplot line. In *Tootsie,* Michael may have been happy to remain as Dorothy for another season, but by falling in love with Julie, he was forced to change the direction of the plot line and to find an opportunity to unmask. In *Witness*, John's care for Rachel on the subplot line raises the stakes on the plot line when Paul holds a gun to her head.

A good subplot not only affects the "A" story by pushing the plot line, but it intersects the plot line. The plot and subplot are connected. They may be connected because the love interest on the subplot line is also the witness on the plot line. They might intersect because the avocation of kayaking on the subplot line becomes the means by which the protagonists escape danger on the plot line (*Deliverance*).

A good subplot carries the theme of the story. In *Dead Poets Society*, each boy has a subplot line that helps expand the theme of creativity and conformity. In *Moonstruck*, each subplot line tells us something more about the theme of love.

Subplots can be about almost anything. Often they're the love story that reveals extra dimensions to the characters. Sometimes they carry important individual themes of identity, integrity, greed, love, or "finding one's self." Sometimes a subplot reveals a character's vulnerability. We often see this in detective films, in which the macho detective has to be strong and prepared for anything on the plot line. But when he's with his girlfriend or mother, we can see his more vulnerable side.

Sometimes, we see a character's goals, dreams, and desires on the subplot line. It's as if the character is too busy "doing" the plot to tell us much about himself or herself. The subplot line gives the character a chance to relax, to dream, to wish, and to think about some larger vision.

The subplot line can show us the transformation of characters. It can show us the beat-by-beat development of a character's identity, self-esteem, or self -confidence. It can help us see why and how a character changes.

Many times, the subplot lines are the most interesting part of a film. In *Witness*, the main plot is somewhat conventional. You've probably seen something like it a hundred times on television detective shows. But the Rachel-John subplot makes the story special and unique. It's what we remember most about the film, what moves us, what interests us.

Think about the Rose-Allnutt subplot in *The African Queen*. The plot is a somewhat conventional war story about blowing up a ship. On the subplot line, we see the memorable moments between Charlie and Rose. We see character transformations, character revelations, and a developing relationship. It is this part of the film that we remember well.

HOW MANY SUBPLOTS DO YOU NEED?

Most films will have at least one ot two subplots. Some films may have as many as five or six. If a film has no subplots, it's in danger of being too linear, without dimensionality. If it has too many, they can muddle the script as well as take time away from the development of the "A" and "B" storylines.

Subplots can work well to complicate a storyline that may be too predictable. *Tootsie* gains many of its complications from the intersection of the subplots. Everytime the story seems to be going in one direction, a surprise comes along as the subplot changes the direction of the plot line. This surprise may be Julie's father falling in love with Dorothy, which forces Michael to have to unmask on the "A" storyline, as well as complicates his relationship with Julie on the "B" storyline. Sandy's friendship with Michael on their subplot line complicates his relationship with Julie on the "B" storyline. Julie's relationship with Ron complicates the relationship of Julie and Dorothy, as well as complicates the "A" story about Michael as Dorothy.

One of the best films to study to see complex subplots in action is *Ruthless People* by Dale Launer. The story gets more and more complicated as every storyline changes the direction of the film. Nothing is as it seems, whether it's the relationship of Barbara (Bette Midler) and her husband Sam (Danny DeVito), or the intentions of the kidnappers, or the relationship of Sam and his mistress, who secretly has another lover, Earl. Each subplot turns the direction of the story, creating humor and unpredictability.

THE STRUCTURE OF SUBPLOTS

Just as the plot line has a beginning, a middle, and an end, so, too, does a subplot line. A good subplot has turning points, a clear set-up, developments, and a payoff at the end. Sometimes the turning points of a subplot reinforce the plot line by occurring right before or right after the turning points of the plot. Sometimes they are separated, where a subplot turning point might happen in the middle of Act Two or Act Three. Sometimes, a subplot doesn't even begin until the first turning point of the plot. In *Tootsie*, the relationship between Julie and Michael begins at the first turning point of the plot line. In *The Fugitive*, Deputy Sam Gerard is introduced at the end of Act One. In *Unforgiven*, Will Munny (Clint Eastwood) and Ned (Morgan Freeman) partner up at the first turning point.

Almost all films have subplots. Some achieve much of their success from a skilled use of these subplots. Three films that use subplots well are *Witness, Back to the Future,* and *Tootsie*. Each of their subplot lines presented unique challenges, yet each was well-structured and added much to the story.

Witness presents a unique use of a subplot. The subplot takes over for part of the story, almost as if it's the plot line. As you remember, the plot line of *Witness* revolves around the central question, "Will John get the killer?" This plot line gives momentum and jeopardy to the film. However, the relational subplot line about John and Rachel becomes the focus of Act Two. Then, in Act Three, we return to the plot line for the final gun battle between John, McFee, and Paul.

The John-Rachel subplot of *Witness* has a clear structure, just like the plot line. The set-up occurs in Act One, when Rachel and John meet. The first turning point occurs at the beginning of Act Two, when Rachel cares for him and he responds to her presence, thereby changing their feelings for each other. Subplot development continues during Act Two, as their relationship develops over breakfast, while dancing, and at the barnraising. A second turning point occurs when they kiss, which raises the stakes of their relationship and raises, again, the central question of the subplot: "Will John and Rachel get together?" A climax occurs when John saves her life by throwing down his gun, and a resolution comes when he says good-bye.

In this subplot, the turning points occur directly after those of the plot line. In this chart, I'm using the minutes in the movie, although this script, like many, equals about one minute to a page. If we were to sketch out the plot line ("A" story) and the subplot line ("B" story), it would look like this:

Set-Up
(A) The murder (15 min.)

(B) Meeting of John and
    Rachel (16 min.)

First Turning Point
(A) Shooting in the garage
    (31 min.)
(B) Rachel cares for John
    (43 min.)

Second Turning Point
(A) John hits punk (85 min.)

(B) John and Rachel kiss
    (91 min.)

Climax
(A) Paul is captured
    (106 min.)
(B) John saves Rachel
    (105 min.)

Resolution
(A) John returns home (109 min.)
(B) John says good-bye. (108 min.)

This unusual use of a subplot can be dangerous, especially since Act Two ordinarily develops the plot and is the focus of the main story. However, in the skillful hands of the writers of *Witness*, we see the various methods they used to keep the plot momentum going in Act Two and to keep us ever mindful of the jeopardy to John from the plot line while focusing on the subplot. During the second act, we return five times to the plot situation. We see scenes in which John telephones his partner to see if he can return. We see his partner interrogated by Paul. And at the end of the second act, we learn that the partner has been killed—which forces John to respond.

In *Back to the Future*, you might remember that the plot line revolved around the time machine and Marty's dilemma about being stuck in the past. The central question of the plot line is, "Will Marty get back to the future?" Here is the basic structure of the plot line:

> Set-up: Marty meets the Professor at the Twin Pines Mall to test his new time machine. (18 min.—remember this is a situational set-up, so it occurs later than in most films.)

> First turning point: By mistake, Marty returns to the past. (30 min.)

> Story development: Marty and the Professor have to figure out a way to get him back to the future.

> Second turning point: Marty and the Professor prepare to capture the lightning, which they hope will return Marty to the future. (76 min.)

> Climax: Marty returns to the future. (106 min.)

As in _Witness_, the subplot of _Back to the Future_ is also a relational story about the unusual courtship and romance of Lorraine and George McFly. Through this subplot, the writers are able to explore the themes of determination, resolution, and transformation. It's a kind of story within a story.

The subplot occurs during Acts Two and Three of the plot, while Marty is back in the past, although important subplot information comes out in Act One. For instance, in Act One, we learned that Lorraine met George because Lorraine's father hit George with a car. We also learned that Lorraine and George first kissed at the "Enchantment Under the Sea" dance, and, at that moment, Lorraine knew that they would spend the rest of their lives together. And we know that Lorraine drinks too much and that George is a slacker.

The set-up of the subplot occurs shortly after Marty returns to the past. Originally, George met Lorraine when her father hit him with the car. But something goes wrong in this dramatic replay of past events in the person of Marty, who jeopardizes his own life by interfering with this first meeting.

EXT.—A RESIDENTIAL STREET—DAY

MARTY comes from around the corner and sees GEORGE'S BIKE parked underneath a tree. Marty looks around, then spots

GEORGE

up in the tree, precariously out on a branch overhanging the street, about twelve feet up. George has a PAIR OF BIN-OCULARS trained on a second-story window in the house across the street.

MARTY

can't figure it out. He moves closer for a better view.

GEORGE focuses the binoculars.

GEORGE'S P.O.V. thru BINOCULARS

of a NAKED GIRL in the second-story bedroom window, dressing.

MARTY

watches in disbelief as he realizes what George is doing.

                    MARTY
          He's a peeping tom!

GEORGE'S P.O.V.

As the girl moves closer to the window.

GEORGE tries to move closer, but loses his balance. He tumbles into the street.

MARTY watches as GEORGE groans, then slowly tries to get up.

Now a CAR comes from around the corner.

George doesn't see it, but Marty can see that it's going to hit George.

> MARTY
> Dad! Look out!

But George is still dazed. Marty dashes into the street and in a spectacular flying leap, knocks him out of the path of the oncoming car.

As Marty moves to avoid the car, the car swerves in the SAME DIRECTION—there's a screech of brakes, and the car hits Marty!

George, never one to get involved, runs off, leaving Marty lying in the street, unconscious.

Well, it's tough luck for George, because with this incident, Lorraine meets Marty instead of George. The story now unfolds differently than expected, as Marty is forced to play matchmaker for his parents, making sure they get together for the dance so that he can be born in the future.

Unfortunately, George is hardly a Don Juan. He resists every suggestion to ask Lorraine to the "Enchantment Under the Sea" dance, so Marty has to put on extra pressure, thus creating the first turning point of the subplot.

INT. GEORGE'S BEDROOM

WE PAN OVER TO GEORGE'S FACE. He's sleeping soundly in bed.

Now, A PAIR OF GLOVED HANDS place FEATHER-WEIGHT HEADPHONES ON George's ears.

THE SAME HANDS now insert a cassette tape labeled "VAN HALEN" into a Walkman. A finger dials the volume level to "10" then presses "PLAY."

GEORGE AWAKENS SCREAMING! He opens his eyes and reacts in further terror: He sees

A FRIGHTENING YELLOW MONSTER . . . Marty in full radiation suit . . . at the foot of his bed!

Marty turns off the music. When he talks, his voice is distorted through the mouth filter in the hood. An open window indicates how Marty got in.

> MARTY
> Silence, Earthling!

> GEORGE
> Who—are you?

> MARTY
> (Imitating Darth Vader)
> My name is Darth Vader. I am an extra-terrestrial from the Planet Vulcan!

> GEORGE
> I must be dreamin'. . .

(. . . .)

> MARTY
> Silence! I am receiving a transmission from the Battlestar Galactica! You, George McFly, have created a rift in the space-time continuum. The Supreme Klingon hereby commands you to take

47

the female earth-person called "Baines, Lorraine" to the location known to you as Hill Valley High School exactly four Earth cycles from now—Saturday night in your language.

> GEORGE
> You mean, take Lorraine to the dance?

> MARTY
> Affirmative.

> GEORGE
> But I don't know if I'll be able to—

MARTY TURNS ON the Walkman again. GEORGE SCREAMS!

And he agrees!

Act Two development of the subplot proceeds, revolving around George's efforts to take Lorraine out—none of which works since she's so involved with Marty. Finally, Marty works out a plan that becomes the second turning point of the subplot line, leading to the kiss at the "Enchantment Under the Sea" dance.

EXT. GEORGE'S BACKYARD—DAY

(. . .)

> MARTY
> Maybe we'd better go over the plan again. Where are you gonna be at 8:55?

> GEORGE
> At the dance.

> MARTY
> And where am I gonna be?

GEORGE
In the parking lot, with her.

MARTY
Okay. So right around 9:00, she's gonna get angry with me—

GEORGE
Why? Why is she gonna get angry with you?

MARTY
(It's hard for him to say)
Well . . . because . . . well, nice girls get angry at guys who . . . who try to take advantage of 'em.

GEORGE
You mean you're gonna—like—touch her on her—

MARTY
George, it's just gonna be an act. Don't worry about it. Just remember that at 9:00, you'll be strolling through the parking lot and you'll see us.
(gulps)
. . . struggling in the car, you'll run over, open the door, and say . . . ?

George doesn't say anything.

MARTY
Your line, George.

GEORGE
Oh. Uh . . . "Hey, you! Get your damn hands off her." You really think I should swear?

> MARTY
> Yes, definitely, George, swear. Then you hit me
> in the stomach, I go down for the count, and
> you and Lorraine live happily ever after.

Here we can feel the energy and urgency begin to build as Marty prepares to head back to the future, but only after he knows that his parents have kissed at the dance. The climax of the subplot line is the kiss, and the resolution occurs immediately afterward, as Marty is leaving.

INT. SCHOOL GYM—BACKSTAGE—NIGHT

> LORRAINE
> Marty, I hope you don't mind, but George asked
> if he could take me home.

(. . .)

> GEORGE
> Marty, will we ever see you again?

> MARTY
> Oh, yeah, I guarantee it!

(. . .)

> LORRAINE
> Marty, it's such a nice name!

And as Marty prepares to leave, he turns for some last instructions:

> MARTY
> By the way, if you ever have a son, and if when
> he's nine years old he burns a hole in the rug,
> go easy on him, O.K.?

And with that, Marty is on his way, back to the future.

If we were to outline this subplot line, it would look like this:

Act One: George doesn't meet Lorraine, so Marty has to get his parents together. Nothing seems to work. George won't ask Lorraine out.

First turning point: Marty dresses as a spaceman to scare George into asking Lorraine to the dance. (47 min.)

Act Two: George tries to court Lorraine. She's only interested in Marty.

Second turning point: Marty and George come up with a plan—George will "save" Lorraine from Marty. (73 min.)

Act Three: In spite of many problems, the plan works.

Climax: George and Lorraine kiss. (86 min.) (Notice: the climax of this subplot occurs shortly after the second turning point of the "A" story.)

Resolution: Marty says good-bye.

The intersection of the subplot and plot line would look like this:

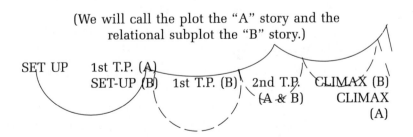

(We will call the plot the "A" story and the relational subplot the "B" story.)

SET UP   1st T.P. (A)
              SET-UP (B)   1st T.P. (B)   2nd T.P.   CLIMAX (B)
                                              (A & B)   CLIMAX
                                                               (A)

This subplot line is unique because it has a double set-up and a double resolution. On the one hand, the subplot in the past has a clear beginning, middle, and end—they meet, the relationship develops, and they get together. But this subplot is framed by the present. In Act One, before Marty leaves for the past, the characters of George and Lorraine are introduced. When Marty returns to the present, we see the second subplot resolution. Marty has transformed them with his presence, and we see quite a different couple. In the second resolution, George and Lorraine have a beautiful home, Biff works for George, and George has just published his first science-fiction novel. Quite a change!

Tootsie presents an example of a very complicated use of subplots. Most films cannot handle more than three subplots, yet *Tootsie* has five.

These are the Michael-Julie subplot, the Michael-Sandy subplot, the Michael-Les subplot, the Michael-Brewster subplot, and the Ron-Julie subplot. Each of these subplots, in some way, has something to say about about the theme of love and friendship. Each has its own structure, and each grows out of and intersects the plot line.

Let's begin by looking at the romantic subplot of *Tootsie* — the relationship between Michael and Julie. Here are the beats of this subplot:

Set-up: Michael (as Dorothy) meets Julie on his first day of work. He's attracted to her. (21 min.)

First turning point: Julie asks him to dinner. Their friendship begins. (46 min.)

Subplot development: They become friends. They go to the country. They talk. Dorothy encourages Julie to break up with Ron. Dorothy helps out Julie by babysitting.

Second turning point: Dorothy tries to kiss Julie. (84 min.)

Development: Julie won't see Dorothy.

Climax: Michael says, "The hard part is over." They've become friends. Now they can continue their relationship. They leave together. (110 min.)

Notice how different this subplot line is from the plot line structure. You might remember the plot structure:

Set-up: Michael can't get a job. (18 min.—Notice: that this is also a situational set-up like *Back to the Future*)

First turning point: Michael gets a job as Dorothy. (20 min.)

Development: Michael becomes very successful.

Second turning point: Michael tries to get out of his contract. "She's" so good that no one will let him out of it. (76 min.)

Climax: Dorothy reveals "herself" to be Michael. (104 min.)

Notice how the romantic subplot dimensionalizes this plot line. The romance is the reason Michael wants to get out of his contract. He's fallen in love; therefore, he no longer wants to be a woman.

In *Tootsie*, the second turning point of the plot happens right after an eleven-minute scene in the country in which Michael falls in love with Julie. As a result of falling in love, he's desperate to stop his charade. But he learns that he's totally stuck in his contract. This puts increased pressure on his desire to express his love to Julie, causing the second subplot turning point to occur (Dorothy tries to kiss Julie). Since Julie won't see him after that (she's "not that kind of girl"), Michael is forced to find some way out of his predicament. This causes the climax of the plot line (the unmasking), which eventually leads to the climax and resolution of the love subplot (they get together).

As you can see, there is movement back and forth from plot to subplot. Without this intersection of plot and subplot, the subplot would seem irrelevent, free-floating, and unrelated to the storyline.

Tootsie is a story based on complications. Subplots are added, one after another, to complicate continually the story-line of "Michael becoming Tootsie"

Certainly, in Michael's opinion, taking a job as an actress should have solved his problem of wanting a job where he could express himself and his talents. Instead, it complicated his whole life. Every subplot line comes out of that strange decision to become a woman and get a job. And every subplot line dimensionalizes the situation and expands the theme of love.

Since the "B" story is the Julie-Michael love story, we might say that the "C" story is the Michael-Sandy subplot, the "D" story the Michael-Les subplot, the "E" story the Michael-Brewster subplot, and the "F" story the Julie-Ron subplot.

If we look at each of them separately, they would look like this:

Michael-Sandy Subplot

(This is the subplot line about Michael's relationship with his insecure friend, Sandy. He has coached her on her acting, encouraged her on her interviews, and been an unromantic friend for years.)

> Set-up: Establishes the long-term friendship between Michael and Sandy by showing them in several situations—at the birthday party and preparing Sandy for an audition. (6 min.)

> First turning point: Michael and Sandy make love, changing the nature of their relationship and putting their friendship in jeopardy. (31 min.)

> Development: Sandy's insecurities increase. She invites Michael to dinner and confronts him about his behavior.

> Second turning point: Sandy discovers that Michael is in love with another woman, and she discontinues their friendship. (94 min.)

Climax: Sandy opens in the new play, and she and Michael are friends again. (106 min.)

Michael-Les Subplot

(Les is Julie's widowed father, who falls in love with Dorothy.)

Set-up: Les meets Dorothy. (42 min.)

First turning point: Les starts to fall in love with Dorothy. (63 min.)

Development: They sing together when Dorothy visits the farm with Julie. Les takes her dancing.

Second turning point: Les proposes. (87 min.)

Climax: Michael gives the ring back. (109 min.)

Resolution: Les forgives him.

Michael-Brewster Subplot

(Brewster is the lecherous doctor on the soap opera who's determined to make love with Dorothy.)

Set-up: Michael is warned that Brewster is a "lech." (34 min.)

First turning point: Brewster begins to be attracted to Dorothy. (40 min.)

Development: They work together. Dorothy tries to avoid Brewster, who keeps trying to kiss her in their scenes.

Second turning point: Brewster sings outside Dorothy's window and makes a pass at her. (88 min.)

Climax: Michael unmasks and Brewster realizes that Dorothy's not a woman. (104 min.)

Julie-Ron Subplot

(Ron is the director of the soap opera and dates Julie—and all sorts of other women behind her back.)

Set-up: Establishes that Julie and Ron are dating. (34 min.)

Development: Michael notices the condescending way Ron treats Julie.

Climax: Julie breaks up with Ron as a result of Dorothy's lessons about self-respect. (79 min.)

Although the "B" story, the main subplot, should have a strong structure to keep it developing and moving throughout the script, other subplots are sometimes better balanced without too much focus on their turning points and their specific structure. Often these smaller subplots (such as the Julie-Ron story) only need a few beats throughout the story to establish them and to bring them into focus so that we can see their influence on the main story.

As in *Tootsie*, many stories have several subplots. Often you hear about the "A" story (the plot) and the "B," "C," and even "D" stories (the subplots).

In many television series, the subplots are an integral part of the form of the series. Many series will have an "A" story, which is the main mystery story (in a detective series), or the main disease story (in a hospital series), or the main problem or situation to be resolved (in a sitcom). The "B" story, then, might be more personal. It might revolve around particular characters' relationships. Perhaps a supporting character falls in love or has a problem with the children. The "C" story in television often adds humor to the story. It might be about the humorous problems of painting the house or redecorating the office or about training the difficult dog. Occasionally a story will have a "D" story that further dimensionalizes the plot line, or it might be a very small character line or storyline of just a few beats.

If the subplot lines are carefully worked out, a good film can work with a great deal of complexity and handle anywhere from three to seven subplots. However, if the story has too many subplots that are not well integrated, it becomes muddy, unfocused, and weighted down with too much going on.

SUBPLOT PROBLEMS

Subplots are responsible for many script problems. Some films have failed because of weak subplot integration. These problems seem to fall into several categories. First of all, many times subplots lack structure. They ramble, they're unfocused, and they disorient the audience so that the audience doesn't know what the story is really about or what's going on.

Sometimes a film has problems because the subplot doesn't intersect the plot and it doesn't seem to have any bearing on the story. Although the subplot might be interesting, it seems to float, unconnected, apart from anything else happening in the story.

Places in the Heart received some criticism of its Vi-Wayne subplot for just this reason. When you watch the film, you'll notice that Vi and Wayne's affair has little to do with Edna's story. Although the subplot has some importance to the theme, it seems separated from the rest of the film.

Some films have problems because of a misplaced subplot. Instead of carrying it throughout the story and interweaving it with the plot, sometimes the subplot is played first. As a result, the plot line begins long after we've become convinced that the subplot is our main story. This happened in *Out of Africa* when the Bror-Karen subplot was almost completely played out before the Karen-Denys plot really got started. This can be disorienting and bewildering to audiences. In the case of *Out of Africa*, it led to a number of critics commenting that Robert Redford came in much too late. And it led to audiences making comments like, "I liked the film, but it took me a long time to get with it."

APPLICATION

As you work with your subplot, separate it from your main storyline so that you can clearly see how it works. If you're not sure which is your "A" story and which is your "B" story, ask yourself, "Where is the movement of the story coming from? Where is the most action?" Chances are, this is your plot line. Then ask yourself, "What is my theme? What do I want to say? What through-lines are helping me to say it?" Chances are, this is your subplot line.

By separating your subplot and plot lines, you can see how you've structured each one of them. Look for the set-up of the subplot. Clarify what happens in Act One, Act Two, and Act Three. Usually, it's more difficult to see clearly the structure of a subplot line. You may need to ask yourself, "What is the development of this subplot?" Once you know that, trace the development back to where it begins. That is probably your first turning point. Then see where the development takes another turn. Is there a place where the subplot becomes more urgent or more intense? If so, this might be the second turning point. Make sure that once the climax of the plot line has happened, the climaxes of the subplot(s) happens quickly.

Making your subplot work is one of the most important jobs of writing. Ask yourself the following questions as you tighten and clarify your rewrite:

Do I need this subplot? Does it add to my story? Does it intersect the story? Does it dimensionalize the story?

How many subplots do I have? If I have more than three or four, are there any that I can cut in order to give more focus to the plot line and the "B" and "C" stories?

Do I have a clear structure for each subplot, with a clear set-up, clear turning points, and a clear climax, particularly for the "B" and "C" stories?

Does my subplot resolution occur close to the climax of the plot line?

If your subplot is tightly structured, if it dimensionalizes the story, and if it intersects the plot, you probably have a workable and dramatic subplot that can go a long way toward helping you say what you want to say. Now the challenge is keeping the script moving, particularly in the difficult second act.

Chapter Four

Act Two—How to Keep It Moving

A ct Two can seem interminable. For writers, it means keeping the story moving for forty-five to sixty pages. For moviegoers, an unworkable second act is a time to snooze, to buy popcorn, and to vow never to see a film by that filmmaker again.

Most Act Two problems come from insufficient momentum and lack of focus. The movie doesn't move! We're unsure what's happening and why.

These related problems develop because the movie has moved off the spine of the story. Unrelated scenes that muddy the story and slow it down have come into the picture. Or the characters are talking, not acting. Or the story is developing too quickly—or too slowly—and is missing or skipping beats.

A clear set-up and Act One development will help the clarity of Act Two. A strong first turning point will do much to keep Act Two moving. But other elements are necessary if the second act is going to keep audiences interested for an hour or more.

WHAT IS SCRIPT MOMENTUM?

Momentum occurs when one scene leads to the next scene, and that scene leads to the next scene. One scene implies the development of the next scene. Or we might say that the seeds of a scene are contained in a previous scene. When scenes are connected in a cause-effect relationship, every scene advances the action, bringing us closer to the climax.

Of course, this is a very simple way of describing something that's very complex. Certainly, some scenes have only small story points and might focus, instead, on subplot or character revelation. Certainly, if every scene were taking us forward in a straight path, always advancing toward the climax, the story would lack subtlety and dimension. But, for right now, think of momentum as coming from action-reaction scenes. As we discuss idea and character, we'll integrate the complexities.

Any good film can demonstrate this cause-effect relationship. Let's look at the end of Act One in *Witness*, when we see strong momentum from scene to scene. The beats move like this:

Samuel points out McFee as the murderer.

As a result, the next scene occurs:

John Book visits Paul and tells him about McFee. Paul tells him to keep quiet about it.

This causes John's reaction:

John returns to his apartment building, only to be shot at by McFee. He realizes that Paul is one of the murderers.

As a result of this shooting, John now takes new action:

John picks up Rachel and Sam, borrows Elaine's car, and drives them to the Amish farm.

This leads to the next scene:

As a result of his injury, John passes out.

This leads into the second act, with John hiding out at the Amish farm.

Notice how every scene is related to the next scene. That's momentum, which continually pushes the story forward.

Action Point

The actions that drive the story forward are called **action points**. An action point is a dramatic event that causes a reaction. Usually this reaction causes another action. Since this action is dramatic and visual (not expressed through dialogue), it pushes the story forward.

We might define an action point as an action that demands a response. In *Tootsie,* Michael hears about a job on a soap opera through Sandy (action). He dresses as a woman and goes to the interview (reaction to the information in the previous scene). The show gives him the job (action). As a result, he meets Julie and is immediately attracted to her (reaction). This mutual interest causes Julie to invite Dorothy for dinner (action) which causes Dorothy/Michael to start falling in love with Julie (reaction).

In each case, the action is visual, dramatic, and strong enough to demand a response of some kind. There could be other actions and reactions that could start another totally different chain of events. What's important here is that there is a connection between scenes. They are not episodic, but each scene comes out of the previous scene, creating a tight story that moves forward to the climax.

Although an action point can be used in any act, they are particularly important in Act Two, where a script needs the most momentum for the longest amount of time. There are several types of action points that can be used. We've already discussed turning points that are action points at the ends of Act One and Act Two and the midpoint scene that occurs in the middle of the script. Other action points include the barrier, the complication, and the reversal.

The Barrier

In many movies, a character tries something—perhaps follows

a clue or performs an action—and it doesn't work because it doesn't lead anywhere. The character has hit a **barrier**. He or she has come up to a brick wall and must change directions and try another action. The barrier is an action point because it forces a character to make a new decision, to take a new action, or to continue on in a new direction.

Notice how barriers work. They stop the action for a moment, and then the character goes around the barrier and continues. The story doesn't develop out of the barrier, it develops out of the decision to try another action. For example, if I were a saleswoman, I might knock on Door 1 to try and sell my product. The customer says, "No." That's a barrier. Then I knock on Door 2 to try to sell my product again. The next customer says, "No." That's another barrier. Finally, I knock on Door 3, and somebody buys. As a result of this sale, I might take off early and celebrate with my boss. In the course of the celebration, my boss gives me a promotion. As a result of my promotion, I get an office and I am no longer selling door-to-door.

Here we can see that the barriers led to further action, but the real development and momentum came as a result of the last action, when the barrier was overcome.

In *Jaws*, we see a good example of barriers at work as Martin, Matt, and Quint try to catch the killer shark:

> First, Quint tries to catch the shark with his line. The shark outwits him and goes under the boat, eventually breaking the line.
>
> Next, they try harpooning the shark, which takes off.
>
> Later, they try the shark cage, but the shark batters it.
>
> Finally, Martin throws the oxygen tank into the shark's mouth and that kills it.

In *Gone With the Wind*, Scarlett tries to get money from Rhett to pay taxes on Tara. When he says "no" (a barrier), she marries Frank Kennedy to accomplish her goal.

In *Witness*, Paul tries to find John at the Amish farm. He calls the Lancaster police, who have no way of locating him because the Amish don't have phones (a barrier). Then Paul questions John's partner, who refuses to talk (a barrier). Eventually, Paul kills the partner, which indirectly causes John Book to reveal where he's hiding.

Barriers can be found in most films. They're used most often in detective stories, mysteries, and action-adventures, and, occasionally, in dramas and comedies. Several in a film can be workable—but if too many are used, the story will feel repetitive, as if it's repeating the action rather than developing the action. In this case, instead of giving the story momentum, it will slow it down. But, if barriers are used sparingly, they can do much to push the story forward.

The Complication

A **complication** is an action point that doesn't pay off immediately. Something happens, but the reaction doesn't come until later. We have to wait for it, and we anticipate the inevitable response.

For instance, let's look at a complication in *Tootsie*: Michael has dressed up as a woman and has become Dorothy Michaels in order to get a job. That was his only intention—to work. But during the first day on the set, he sees Julie. Nothing happens immediately, but we know that it will. Julie's presence has complicated Michael's intention. We guess that he will fall in love with Julie, which will jeopardize his work.

The meeting and the response are thirty-two pages apart. Dorothy meets Julie on page twenty-nine. At their first meeting, they simply notice each other.

> RITA
> Ron. I want to test Ms. Michaels. We're going
> to run some tape on her.

JULIE PHILIPS, pretty, blonde, the show's leading lady, passes as Dorothy drops the "sides." She kneels quickly to retrieve them and discovers Julie kneeling beside her, helping.

DOROTHY
Oh, dear, I can't find page four.

JULIE
They'll never know the difference.

Julie has gathered the pages. They both stand up. Julie hands Dorothy the pages, smiling understandingly.

JULIE
Don't think of it as a camera, think of it as something friendly, like a cannon.

And she moves away, Dorothy staring after. At the door Julie turns, winks, gives a "thumbs up" gesture.

Nothing happens with this first meeting, but from Dorothy's look at Julie, we know "he's" smitten with her.

Thirty-two pages later. Julie asks "her" on the first date:

JULIE
Dorothy . . . I know this is just what you want to hear but—we've got twenty-six pages tomorrow. If you could find it in your heart to come over and run it with me; we could have something to eat. I'm a born defroster. Surely, you can't tell me you've had enough soap opera for today.

The relationship grows from the complication (the meeting), leading to the response (the date).

In *Tootsie*, we see another complication when Brewster, the soap-opera doctor, meets Dorothy and decides that he wants her. Again, the payoff of this action point isn't immediate. It happens far into Act Three, when he comes to serenade Dorothy and forces her to receive his affections.

Further complications happen when Julie's father falls in love with Dorothy. He meets her early in Act Two, but little develops until Dorothy visits his farm at the end of the act. They sing together, dance together, and that leads to the proposal.

A complication is not your ordinary garden-variety action point. It's actually quite rare. You don't see it in many scripts. Sometimes, when it's there, it's quite subtle. In looking for a complication, check for three elements:

> A complication doesn't pay off immediately, so it adds anticipation to the story.

> A complication is the beginning of a new through-line or subplot. It doesn't turn the story around; instead, it keeps the story moving forward, but with a new twist.

> A complication gets in the way of a character's intention.

Because of Julie, Brewster, and Les, Michael can't continue to be Dorothy Michaels, even though his career is blossoming. His original intention—to be successful—continues. These people haven't interfered with his overall intention. But they have interfered with his willingness to continue as Dorothy. And that's the complication.

The Reversal

The strongest kind of action point is a **reversal**. A reversal changes the direction of the story 180 degrees. It makes the story move from a positive to a negative direction, or from a negative to a positive direction. It's stronger than most turning points, which only turn the action in another direction but do not reverse it. A reversal is a complete turnaround.

Reversals can work physically or emotionally. They can reverse the action or reverse a character's emotions. In *Ghostbusters*, our unemployed university professors reverse direction and start their own business. In *Jaws*, the townspeople think that they've caught the shark and start celebrating, but the celebration is reversed when Matt informs them that the captured shark isn't the killer.

In *Cocoon*, Walter's mission seems destroyed when the old people drain the energy from the swimming pool and one of the Anterians dies. It reverses his mission. But his mission is reversed again when the old people offer to help save the cocoons.

All three of these moments are also emotional reversals. The down and out pyschic professors in *Ghostbusters* suddenly change from disappointed to excited. In *Jaws*, Martin and Matt move from celebration to fear. And Walter, in *Cocoon*, moves from grief and despair to hope.

Playing a reversal at the first or second turning point can be a particularly good way to build momentum into the second and third acts. But reversals can work anywhere. In a horror film, we often see a reversal happen when everyone is celebrating and feeling safe and the monster suddenly appears at the window.

In a detective film, we see a reversal when the discouraged detective suddenly puts two and two together and realizes how to solve the case.

In a romance, we see reversals at work when the lost soldier unexpectedly returns to his beloved or when the beloved one, on her deathbed, suddenly recovers.

Whereas a barrier pushes the story forward by forcing new decisions, and a complication pushes the story forward by leading to an anticipated payoff, a reversal catapults the story by forcing it to take a new direction that causes new development. Because it creates such momentum, you rarely need more than a couple of reversals in a script. One or two will have the power to push the story through that difficult second act. In all of these examples, the action develops, rather than repeats, itself.

Instead of having a scene in which a detective asks the same question over and over again, the detective asks the question often enough to make a point (usually two or three times), but not so often that it repeats the same action. Then the story can develop further, to different investigations, different discoveries, different actions.

The Scene Sequence

Momentum is gained through action points. These create action-reaction scenes where each scene leads to the next, advancing the story to the climax.

Occasionally, these action-reaction scenes are grouped together around one central mini-storyline. These scenes create a beginning, middle, and end, setting up the situation, building it, and reaching a climax without any interruption from subplots.This type of scene offers the most momentum and is called a **scene sequence**.

Most scene sequences are relatively short, ranging from about three to seven minutes. Occasionally, a scene sequence might form the entire third act, as in *Witness*, when the final battle scene is made up of one long, fourteen-minute scene sequence.

Many of the most memorable scenes from films are scene sequences. The burning of Atlanta in *Gone With the Wind* is a seven-minute scene sequence. The storm scene in *Places in the Heart* is a seven-minute scene sequence. The last battle in *Star Wars* is a scene sequence,

In *Gone With the Wind*, we have two separate scene sequences in a row. The first is "Melanie has her baby," and the second is "Atlanta burns." Both are about seven minutes long, and they are probably two of the most memorable scenes in the entire film. By looking at these two, we can see how a scene sequence works to give focus and momentum to the story.

"Melanie has her baby" begins after the seige of Atlanta has lasted for thirty-five days. Knowing that Atlanta will be taken by the Yankees, the soldiers and townspeople begin to leave the city. Just at this time, Melanie announces her labor pains.

Set-up: Melanie announces that she has labor pains.

First turning point: Scarlett sends Prissy for the doctor.

Development: Prissy returns, saying the doctor can't come.

Second turning point: Scarlett is told she must deliver the baby.

Climax: Melanie's baby is delivered.

The "Atlanta burns" sequence works in the same way:

Set-up: Prissy comes to get Rhett, asking him to help them escape.

First turning point: Rhett comes to take them away.

Development: Men try to stop their carriage, the crowds try to get the horse, and Rhett announces that they must get past the depot before it explodes.

Second turning point: They come to the ammunition depot, which is already burning. This puts their escape in jeopardy.

Development: They escape through the flames.

Climax: They get through, just as the depot explodes.

Resolution: They reach safety, and Rhett leaves.

Scene sequences, like any action point, can come at any place in the story. Many times a scene sequence happens shortly after the middle of Act Two, when the act is in danger of lagging. Occasionally, a scene sequence is found in Act One, either as a very exciting beginning set-up (you'll find these sequences at the beginning of many James Bond films), or to take us toward the first turning point.

Steven Speilberg, that modern master of momentum, often uses scene sequences. You'll find a short one in *Back to the Future,* when Biff chases Marty and drives into a truckload of manure. In *Jaws*, there are several scene sequences, such as the "Harpooning the shark" sequence, the "Using the shark cage" sequence, and the final "Victory" sequence. In *Schindler's List*, there are several scene sequences, including "The Killing in the Ghetto," "The Amon the Good" sequence, and "The Moving to Czechoslavakia" scene sequence.

This does not mean that Spielberg imposes scene sequences on his script. I doubt that Spielberg wakes up in the morning and says, "I'm going to make me a scene sequence today." However, Spielberg, like many of the best storytellers, has an instinctive feel for sequences because he has an instinct for momentum. Sometimes, however, that instinct has to be consciously trained.

PROBLEMS IN MOMENTUM

The lack of momentum is one of the most common problems in films. Usually these problems occur because there's not a clear three-act structure with clear turning points to keep the story moving. Sometimes they occur because certain scenes take the story on a tangent, rather than keeping it focused on the storyline.

Often, momentum problems are misdiagnosed. As a result, the solution doesn't solve the problem.

Most filmmakers try to solve momentum problems by adding more action to the story. It's not unusual to watch a television detective series that adds a car chase, a fist fight, or a shootout every time the story seems to slow down. Unfortunately, these kinds of actions rarely solve the problem. Often, they get the story off its spine, thereby slowing momentum even more, especially after the action is finished.

Sometimes, filmmakers confuse momentum with pacing. To solve a momentum problem, they pick up the pace of the story, sometimes hurrying the plot to the extent that there's no let-up for the audience. If the pace is too fast, the audience can't catch up with the story. Therefore, instead of being "with" the story, the audience feels as if the story is always ahead of them.

Sometimes, when audiences lose interest in a story, it might look as if the problem is a lack of momentum. Actually, the problem may have little to do with story movement. If a story is too predictable, audiences will lose interest. If there are no subplots to dimensionalize the story, or if the characters are stereotypes who fail to involve us, interest will also diminish.

In these cases, focusing on the development of the plot line, subplot, and theme will pick up interest, provided this development combines with strong momentum.

APPLICATION

None of these tools of rewriting can be imposed on a script. They need to be integral to the story. But all of these elements can strengthen a script that almost has a reversal in it, or a complication, or a scene sequence.

In order to use these elements in a script, it's important to understand them. You might start doing this by watching films specifically to identify these elements. Many films rely more on one element than another. Some use all of them!

Just for starters, notice the number of barriers that Sam Gerard encounters while trying to find Richard Kimble in *The Fugitive.*

Notice the use of reversals in *Ghostbusters* (such as when the EPA man lets the ghost out), or in *Fatal Attraction* when the sexually exciting second night turns into a suicide attempt.

Notice the use of strongly structured scenes with beginnings, middles, and ends, such as the first long scene in the restaurant in *Schindler's List*, or some of the long fight sequences in *Shane.*

Once you're clear how these elements are used in particular films, it will be much easier to find and develop them within your own script.

Sometimes, scene sequences can be created after the first draft with very little rewriting. Many times, action-reaction scenes revolve around several ideas rather than one. To create a scene sequence, the writer can find the scenes related to one idea and string them together to create a set-up, development, and climax to the sequence.

A reversal can often be created by punching up and strengthening an action point. Think about the suddenness when the *Ghostbusters* lose their jobs just when they've finally seen a ghost in the library. If this had been played without the reversal, we would have seen the men drift back to their office and talk a bit, followed by someone drifting in to tell them that they might lose their jobs. We might have all drifted out of the theater while waiting for some punch. Instead, this moment was played quickly as a physical and emotional reversal, catapulting the story forward.

You can create strong emotional reversals by looking for emotional moments that can be expanded or extended. If your main character is "kind of sad" before moving to "sort of happy," see if you can create "despair leading to ecstasy" for greater punch. Or reverse to the negative, moving from celebration to horror or fear.

In summary, look at your script and ask yourself:

How are action points used? Is the story gaining momentum through action points, or does it use dialogue to push the story forward?

What kinds of action points are within my script? Barriers? Complications? Reversals? Where do they occur, and how often?

Are there any scene sequences, or potential scene sequences, in the script? Where do they occur? How are they working to give energy to the story?

Does my script go off on tangents, or does it stay focused on plot and subplot development?

Can I construct action points or scene sequences from the dramatic elements I'm already using in my story?

Above all, remember that as long as there are actions and responses that are related to your storyline, your script will continue to move. You do not need big actions to move your story. Not every physical action needs a dramatic physical response to move your story. At times, you can move your story through physical actions, through dialogue, or through emotional responses. As long as there are connections between one action and another, and as long as you have a structure that supports your story, your script will move.

Keeping this concept in mind, you needn't be concerned if your script is relational and slower paced than *Rambo* or a James Bond film, or if your fast-paced action-adventure slows down for a love scene. As long as there are action-reaction scenes, your script will have direction, focus, and momentum.

Analyze what kinds of action points you use and how you keep the story moving in Act Two. Don't impose something on your story if it's not intrinsic, but don't be afraid to be strong and dramatic. The story, and particularly the second act, will need energy and punch to keep it exciting—and to keep momentum flowing.

Chapter Five

Creating the Scene

S cenes are the building blocks of the story. Through the use of images and dialogue, a great scene advances the story, reveals character, explores an idea, and builds an image. A great scene will do all of these. A good scene will do more than one.

Many times writers have said to me, "I wrote that scene to reveal character." And that's all the scene is doing. But film is dimensional. A scene can accomplish many purposes, all at the same time. The background might be showing an image. The actions might reveal character. A piece of dialogue might advance the story. And the combination of all of these can explore the theme.

Great scenes can build tension and suspense, move an audience to tears or terror, even cause physical changes to happen in the audience from sweaty palms to a faster heart rate.

A great scene involves the audience emotionally.

Aristotle said that tragedy should engender pity and fear. And certainly many of the best films will awaken those emotions. But they'll also bring out other feelings—such as compassion, joy, sometimes anger and frustration, excitement, disappointment, and sadness.

THE IDEA OF THE SCENE

As with all other aspects of screenwriting, there are not rules and formulas, but concepts and ideas that can help you understand dramatic writing. As you work on your scenes, remember there is a reason why film is called "moving pictures." Although writing implies words, the screenwriter is actually creating dialogue <u>and</u> images. This means that the writer is choosing scenes that contain movement and direction—as well as conflict, action, and emotions—all expressed through cinematic locations, dramatic actions, and dynamic character relationships.

Since films move, most scenes are short—anywhere from a sentence or two or as many as three or four pages. Dialogue tends to be spare, moving back and forth between characters with just a few sentences for each speech. Since there is a limit to the script—usually it's only about 120 pages—every line of dialogue and every description needs to count. And since the scene is going to be expressed by the director and actors, the scenes need to imply the color and textures and relationships and feelings that can be brought to life by these other artists. When writing a script, the words that you select really need to count. Many details need to be conveyed in just a few well-chosen sentences to paint the picture of the characters and actions, while not telling so much that you're actually doing everybody else's job.

A good scene accomplishes a number of objectives:

(1) It advances the story, giving you the information you need to follow the story. It might advance the story by giving you clues in a mystery, by developing a relationship in a love story, by taking you on a journey where each scene gets you closer to your destination. In a good script, scenes take you in a direction, and a good proportion of the scenes will move you closer to the climax. (Think about how the

scenes build information in a film like *The Fugitive*, or move Michael closer to his unmasking in *Tootsie*, or give Clarise Starling more clues in *The Silence of the Lambs*.)

A story scene implies that other action will follow in the next scene. It anticipates the action that will follow. It sets up and contains the seeds of the next scene within the current scene.

In *Witness*, a story scene shows John Book getting information from Samuel that will advance the action:

> JOHN BOOK
> I'm a police officer . . . It's my job to find out what happened. I want you to tell me everything you saw when you went in there.

And out of this scene the investigation proceeds.

A story scene doesn't need to be direct or on the nose, as long as it implies another scene.

In *Tootsie*, George the agent says to Michael:

> GEORGE
> No one will hire you.

> MICHAEL
> No one? You mean no one in . . .

> GEORGE
> (interrupting)
> No one anywhere.

CUT TO:

EXT: STREET—DAY

And the story begins as we see Michael, as Dorothy, walking down the street on his first pair of high heels. If no one will hire Michael as Michael, maybe they'll hire him as Dorothy Michaels.

> (2) A scene reveals character. Most character revelation occurs in subplot scenes, but "A" story scenes can also reveal character by showing how someone makes decisions, what kind of actions are chosen, how a character operates under pressure.

Character information in a "B" story scene can often pay off in an "A" story scene. Sometimes a scene might seem to only be about revealing character, but might introduce some ability that will be useful as the protagonist gains the goal.

Perhaps we see a protagonist taking part in his favorite sport—rock climbing. It seems as if this is just a character revelation scene, but later we see that the protagonist needs this skill when he has to rescue the MIAs or storm the fortress at the top of the cliff.

The best character revelatory scenes don't choose character details by happenstance, but reveal character traits that can pay off in some other part of the script. So the character details that you give your character in one scene, such as a love of computer games (*WarGames*) an ability to imitate different voices (*Mrs. Doubtfire*), or a love of playing the piano (*The Piano*), are not simply there for character revelation, but act also to advance the story.

In *Witness*, we discover new aspects about John and Rachel when she brings him lemonade in the barn. The scene functions on a number of levels. It tells us that he's a good carpenter, thereby setting up the barn-raising scene. It contrasts the characters of John and Daniel through the way they both drink lemonade. Daniel is a civilized sipper, John is a sensual gulper. It develops their relationship through his teasing of her. And it advances the "B" story by showing that Rachel is clearly more intrigued by John than by Daniel.

> JOHN BOOK
> What happened to Hochstetler?

> RACHEL
> He had some lemonade and he left.

> JOHN BOOK
> A real fireball.

> RACHEL
> You know carpentry?

> JOHN
> . . . Some . . .

> RACHEL
> Can you do anything else?

> JOHN
> Whacking. I'm hell at whacking.

Here the teasing dialogue reveals the dynamic between these two which is, at this point, all beneath the surface. As in all great scenes, there is a subtext that is being played here. We might phrase Rachel's subtext as: "I'm attracted to you and I want you to be clear that I'm not attracted to Daniel." For John, the subtext might be: "I sense the relationship between you and Daniel is not the passion of the century. I want to check that out, but I don't want to get too intimate here because I'm going to need to leave soon." The attraction that is developing here, culminates with the dance in the barn and the barnraising scene.

    (3) A scene also explores a theme. Movies are about something. They may be about good and evil or about identity or integrity or greed or love or betrayal or any number of ideas that relate to the human condition. Scenes explore and expand upon an idea

through words that the character says, actions they take, and through the images created in the script.

Sometimes a scene might tell the theme right out. In *Witness*, Eli explains a central idea of Amish philosophy:

> ELI
> This gun of the hand is for the taking of human life . . . What you take into your hands, you take into your heart.

Other times, the idea is expressed through decisions and reactions of a character. Rachel expresses her philosophy and values through her actions.

Book's big .38 revolver lies holstered in the drawer. Fascinated, Samuel picks it up. Unable to resist, he starts to remove the weapon.

> BOOK
> Stop . . . Never, ever point a loaded gun . . .

And when Rachel comes in—

> RACHEL
> Samuel, wait for me downstairs. John Book, as long as you are in this house, I insist that you follow our laws.

> BOOK
> Here, take it. Put it somewhere he won't find it.

A beat, then Rachel takes the pistol, holding it tentatively, and starts to go.

Here, the attitudes and situation carry the theme of nonviolence.

(4) A good scene also builds an image. Although some of this is the work of the director, the writer needs to include images in the script, and be conscious that images mean something.

When done poorly, an image merely repeats an idea, rather than develops an idea. A stagnant or repetitive image might be an image of greed that shows a character hoarding his money. Each scene repeats this image, perhaps showing us a number of scenes of a character counting money to show that a character is greedy.

But a developing image expands the image. To build an image of greed, the writer might show a person willing to do anything to make money. The next scene might show the person buying expensive furnishings or jewelry. Another scene might show guards, alarms, dogs who protect the wealth. Later, a scene might show the person putting money above family, relationships, and personal integrity.

Sometimes an image carries the theme visually within a scene.

These might be descriptions that set the theme of community, as in the first scene in *Witness*: "Black-clad figures makes their way down a lane"—showing a community that is alike in values, dress, and lifestyle.

Ideally, a scene will advance the story, reveal character, explore a theme, and build an image. But rarely will a scene reach this ideal. Some scenes in a mystery might only advance the story and give some small character revelation. Some subplot scenes might not advance the story, but will concentrate on character and theme. But keeping in mind that scenes can work on many levels will automatically improve the quality of the scenes you choose to show.

WHICH SCENES TO USE, WHERE SHOULD YOU PUT THEM?

Any story contains an infinite number of potential scenes as characters move through the story. Characters sleep, eat, get up in the morning, interact with each others, argue, make decisions, strategize future events, take part in leisure-time activities—the list is endless. How does a writer choose which ones to use?

To a great extent, you can trust your dramatic instincts. But there are some ideas to keep in mind as you create scenes.

Make sure that the beats to the "A" story are clear. Every story has beats that are part of the story spine. Although you may not show every beat, you will need to map them out in an outline to make sure that your story adds up. In a murder mystery, there's the murder, the investigator taking the case, specific discoveries made along the way, and capturing the bad guy at the end. In a comedy such as *Tootsie*, it's necessary to show the events that establish that Michael can't get a job, to build specific moments that show that Michael is an excellent actor as Dorothy, to show the complication as he falls in love with Julie at the same time that the show wants to renew his contract, and then to clearly show how he works it out. Of course, also map out the beats of your subplots so that all of the storylines track from beginning to end. You want to make sure that you don't have story holes by checking of all your scenes to make sure that they contain the story beats that you need to tell your story.

Show, rather than talk about, the action. Film is about action. It's about a series of events that move us forward toward the climax. Rather than talk about the murder, or a promotion, or a meeting between lovers, it gains immediacy, if you show it. As you outline your story, find those events that create the most cinematic story, and put them on screen. And show them in the most dramatic way possible.

Make static scenes interesting by adding action. Often you

will have scenes that are static, such as driving in a car or sitting in a restaurant. Even these scenes can be made intense, interesting, dramatic, and revelatory.

In many movies, we see static scenes with some activity added to them. Think of how often you see a scene where we get valuable information while characters work in their garden, shell peas, weed the hydrangeas, fold the laundry, or where the woman brushes her hair before bed.

In *Fatal Attraction*, there's a scene where Dan and Beth need to talk about the house they want to buy. It's a static exposition scene that takes place in the kitchen. But added to the scene are the charming card tricks that Ellen tries to perform for her Dad, usually getting them wrong.

Even though the scene is about boring exposition, the writer can make something interesting happen in the scene.

Use scenes to orient the audience. There are times that you need to add Establishing scenes to let the audience know where they are, or the relationship of one element to another. Generally an establishing scene is brief. It might show the car driving up to the apartment building to establish where the character lives, or a brief scene that establishes the outside of the prison, followed by a short interior scene to show the arrangement of cells. Sometimes an establishing scene shows the height of the dam (*The Fugitive*) or how long the race will be (*Ben Hur*) or how high the tower is (*Vertigo*). Without these scenes, the audience can be disoriented and will lack the visual information they need to understand the story. (If you want to see films that don't have sufficient establishing scenes, watch *Mrs. Soffel* or the gunfight at the O.K. Corral in the film *My Darling Clementine*. In both these films, many times we don't know where we are and don't know physical proximity of people and buildings and horses.)

Montages can be used to give information and show passage of time. A montage is a series of short scenes that generally give one piece of information in a scene. Generally, they are without dialogue, although some montages may have one or two spoken lines. By doing several very short scenes in a row, information can be conveyed quickly.

You've all seen montages of characters falling in love—they have a candlelight dinner, walk on the beach hand-in-hand, kiss under a full moon, with the final scene of them passionately making love. Instead of spending an entire act to show them falling in love, these montages show them falling in love over a period of a few seconds so that the story can develop other aspects of their relationship (what happens after they've fallen in love, perhaps focusing on their marriage). Although these romantic montages are the most popular and overused montages, a montage can be about anything—a series of scenes about finding a job, about building a house, moving to a new city, or investigating a crime.

Montages, however, are not developed scenes. They don't show much character interaction. They don't express conflict. They don't convey much emotion. But they do get through material quickly. You may want to watch the montage at the beginning of Act Two in *Ghostbusters*, when the ghosts are finally successful. It begins right after they've captured the ghost in the hotel. The montage shows them being talked about on the street, appearing on the cover of *Time* Magazine, and even discussed on the Larry King Show.

The Fugitive has a very workable montage about the middle of Act Two when the marshalls are questioning Richard's friends, and Richard is preparing his new identity as a hospital janitor.

In *Tootsie*, there is a montage at the end of Act Two that shows Dorothy having trouble taking care of Amy, Julie's child. The montage shows the passing of a long, difficult evening.

MONTAGE:

INT. AMY'S BEDROOM—LATER
Sitting on floor, encircled by all of Amy's toys, Dorothy jiggles toys at her, makes "happy" faces. Amy continues to cry.

INT. LIVING ROOM—LATER
Dorothy jogging around the room in her high heels, holding Amy as she continues to cry. She jogs from the living room to the foyer toward the bedroom.

INT. KITCHEN—LATER
Dorothy feeding Amy applesauce (they are both covered with it). Amy still cries. Dorothy is hit by food that Amy throws back.

INT. BATHROOM—LATER
Dorothy tries to clean her blouse and hair, while talking to Amy whom she has placed in the sink.

INT. LIVING ROOM—LATER
Dorothy sits with Amy on her lap and uses the toys on the table to try to get Amy to fall asleep. Nothing seems to work.

INT. AMY'S BEDROOM—LATER
AMY plays amid toys on the floor. CAMERA PULLS BACK to reveal Dorothy asleep in the corner. Dorothy wakes up with a start to O.S. noise, gets up and begins to pick up Amy.

IF YOU HAVE TO DO EXPOSITION SCENES, KEEP THEM VISUAL AND DRAMATIC.

There are times that the audience needs to have certain information in a scene, and it's simply not interesting. Even here, there are a number of techniques you can use to compensate for what could be a static, boring scene.

One of the best exposition scenes can be found in *Raiders of the Lost Ark*. As you read the scene, notice the number of techniques in this scene that cover up the fact that its function is really to tell you one piece of information—the Nazis have discovered Tanis.

If you re-watch the film, you'll see that this scene could have taken place almost anywhere—in an office, a small classroom, a sterile lecture room. Instead, it uses a visually interesting setting—a large gothic-type lecture hall adds visual interest to the scene.

INT.—LECTURE HALL—DAY

INDY steps onto a platform in the front of the room. Two men, EATON and MUSGROVE, follow him.

> EATON
> You studied under Professor Ravenwood at the
> University of Chicago.

> INDY
> Yes. I did.

> EATON
> You have any idea of his present whereabouts?

> INDY
> Just rumors, really, somewhere in Asia, I think.
> I haven't spoken to him for ten years. We were
> friends, but, uh . . . had a bit of a falling out,
> I'm afraid.

This begins the backstory information that is going to reveal character information throughout the scene. Here we find out where Indy went to school. (And we discover that the writers have done their research, choosing one of the best schools in the country for Indy's Ph.D. This man is smart!) We discover information about his relationship with Dr. Ravenwood. But the information isn't just given to us as information, it's given to us with an attitude. Indy clearly doesn't feel good about the falling out with Ravenwood.

As the scene proceeds, it shades in a sense of mystery as well as the important exposition information that sets up the entire story.

> MUSGROVE
> Dr. Jones, now you must understand that this is all strictly confidential.

> INDY
> I understand.

Musgrove clears his throat.

> MUSGROVE
> Yesterday afternoon our European sections intercepted a German communique that was sent from Cairo to Berlin. Now . . .

> EATON
> (interrupting)
> See, over the last two years, the Nazis have had teams of archeologists running around the whole world looking for all kinds of religious artifacts. Hitler's a nut on the subject . . . He's obsessed with the occult. And right now, apparently there's some kind of German archeological dig going on in the desert outside Cairo.

Musgrove opens a briefcase.

> MUSGROVE
> Now we've got some information here, but we can't make anything out of it and maybe you can. (He reads) "Tanis development proceed-

ing. Acquire headpiece, Staff of Ra. Abner
Ravenwood, U.S."

Here again is a great deal of exposition. But notice how the
dialogue moves back and forth between Brody and Musgrove,
keeping up the interest by bouncing back and forth. And notice how the excitement builds as Eaton interrupts Musgrove
so that he can be the one to tell Indy the important information, but Musgrove, who is the keeper of the telegram, gets the
floor once more to get to the point of why they're there.

As the scene proceeds, Indy's emotional reaction to this
information further shades the scene. He's clearly excited about
the information. He even interrupts Brody as the information
spills out.

     Indy and Brody exchange a glance. Indy thumps the
table with his hand.

               INDY
    The Nazis have discovered Tanis.

              EATON
    Just what does that mean to you—Tanis?

              BRODY
    Well, ah . . .

              INDY
    (interrupting)
    The city of Tanis is one of the possible resting
    places of The Lost Ark.

            MUSGROVE
    The Lost Ark?

We also begin to get information about Indy's vast reservoir of knowledge. Although he doesn't consider himself the expert on Tanis . . . ("Ravenwood did the first serious work on Tanis. It was his obsession really. But he never found the city.")

Previously, the scene has established Indy's archaeological skills. Now Indy's professorial skills begin to shine.

> INDY
> The Ark of the Covenant, the chest the Hebrews used to carry around the Ten Commandments in.

> EATON
> . . . You mean THE Ten Commandments?

> INDY
> Yes, the actual Ten Commandments. The original stone tablets that Moses brought down out of Mount Horeb and smashed, if you believe in that sort of thing.

The men are impressed but impassive.

> INDY
> Either of you guys go to Sunday school? . . .

Here we get more story information, but also more character information about Indy's attitude toward religion. He went to Sunday school, but now seems to be agnostic.

The scene then proceeds to explain the history of the Ark, how it was placed in the Temple of Solomon in Jerusalem, and then disappeared in a sandstorm.

But there's more information to get across. It does this through the use of strong visuals.

> EATON
> What exactly is a headpiece to the Staff of Ra?

INDY
Well, the staff is just a stick.

He indicates the height, then flips a blackboard and starts to draw on it with a piece of chalk.

This visual helps us recognize the staff when we see it later in the film.

And, at the end of the scene, a picture helps symbolize the power of the Ark.

EATON
What does this Ark look like?

INDY
I've got a picture of it right here. That's it.

He opens a latched book to an engraving. It shows a Biblical battle—the Israelite Army is vanquishing an opposition force. The most astounding thing is the brilliant jet of white light and flame (coming from the Ark) . . .

And the scene moves toward the end with a bit of humor, a good rejoinder from Brody.

EATON
Good God.

BRODY
Yes, that's just what the Hebrews thought.

MUSGROVE
Well now, what's that supposed to be coming out of there?

INDY
Lightning, fire . . . power of God or something.

> EATON
> I'm beginning to understand Hitler's interest in
> this thing.

> BRODY
> Oh, yes. The Bible speaks of the Ark leveling
> mountains and laying waste to entire regions.
> An army which carries the Ark before it is in-
> vincible.

And the scene ends with a sense of what's at stake if the Nazis really have discovered Tanis.

Throughout the scene, emotions, attitudes, visuals, and conflict have made this watchable and cinematic while still accomplishing its purpose—to give information in a dramatic way.

FROM WHOSE POINT-OF-VIEW?

Early in your decision-making about scenes, you'll need to decide: "Whose story is it? Who do I care about, identify with, follow in this film? To what extent do I see the story through a specific person's point-of-view?"

A film can be told through one character's point-of-view, through several characters' points-of-view, or through an omniscient point-of-view. Many films want you to identify wholeheartedly with a particular character. You only know what the character knows. Every scene contains that character, and you are seeing the story through the character's eyes. *Tootsie* is about Michael Dorsey. Virtually every scene is about Michael. We follow him throughout the film. *The African Queen* is told through the point-of-view of two characters, Rose and Allnutt. Every scene contains one or the other character.

An omniscient point-of-view lets the audience in on information that the protagonist couldn't know. It gives a broader, more objective view of the story. Instead of identifying totally with one character, we see other elements of the story. *Schindler's List* has an omniscient point-of-view, as we see scenes that focus on Schindler. on the Commandant, on the women in the concentration camp, on the children, the men, the Nazis, the people in the ghetto, etc.

Sometimes detective films want the audience to know more than the protagonist, so there are scenes with the villain, perhaps with the police, even though most of the scenes will still focus on the protagonist.

Some films have a one- or two-person point-of-view combined with some omniscient scenes. In *The Fugitive*, most scenes are either about Deputy Gerard or Richard Kimble, but there are a few scenes with other characters, such as the Chicago police, the one-armed man, a few scenes where marshalls are in a scene without Gerard. If you want the audience to identify strongly with one or two characters, you'll have a narrower, subjective point-of-view. If you need to show more information for the audience to understand the many story beats that make up the mystery, you'll broaden the point-of-view.

WHERE TO START THE SCENE? WHERE TO END THE SCENE?

Some scenes begin too early. They lag. They dawdle. They don't seem to have a clear focus. They don't know where they're going or how to get there.

Other scenes begin too late. They don't give the audience the important information they need to understand the scene. They don't have adequate time to build tension, conflict, or suspense.

In order to decide where to start the scene, first begin by deciding where to end the scene. What is the point of the scene? Why include the scene? What's the most important information the audience needs to get from the scene? What is its focus? Where is it heading?

A scene might be about Tootsie getting the job, with the hiring as the point of the scene. A scene might build to a murder. It might be about a detective finding important information. This goal of the scene is going to occur at the end of the scene.

Now where to begin? What does the audience need to know in order to understand the scene? That's the set-up of the scene. In *Tootsie*, the scene might begin with Tootsie arriving at the studio. Here, the context of the studio would be established at the beginning of the scene. This context includes a sense of the competition, the establishing of the people involved, information about what is asked of Dorothy.

Then, what is the development of the scene? What events are necessary in order to take us from the set-up to the climax of the scene? In *Tootsie*, the development includes reading, almost being dismissed, and then finally hiring her.

Think about where the scene needs to go in order to link up with the next scene. In Tootsie, the hiring scene leads directly to Michael, as Dorothy, greeting her agent at the Russian Tea Room, proving that he can get the job.

Think about the action of the scene. Many writers will think in terms of the information of the scene, and the scenes will become chatty, talking about information. But if you think about the action of the scene, automatically the scene will get new energy. It will contain events that force reactions and decisions and new actions, and things will start happening. Maybe a scene originally shows people talking at a dinner party. It might talk about, rather than show. If you re-think the scene in terms of what is happening, you may decide to start the scene by showing people meeting and reacting to each other. Or maybe you'll decide that the scene is about a conflict and confrontation that happens between two guests, which leads to some action. (One guest leaves in disgust? They become more heated? Someone throws their wine glass?) By thinking about the action of the scene—even a relatively static scene—the scene will become dramatic, emotional, and dynamic.

STRUCTURE AND SHAPE YOUR SCENES

Just as the overall story has structure, scenes also have shape. They have direction. They have movement. And a well-structured scene will often have its three acts, with a clear beginning, middle, and end, and often a first and second turning point, and a dramatic build to the climax.

One of the best-structured scenes is the murder scene in *Witness*. I have slightly edited the scene here, but in the script it's approximately three pages long and about three-and-a-half minutes on the screen. In the film, you can see how Peter Weir's direction reinforces the intrinsic three-act structure of the written scene by changing the movement and sound at the turning points.

As I write out the scene, I will be dividing it into three acts so that you can more clearly understand the structure of the scene.

ACT ONE: (The idea of the beginning of the scene is to show Samuel entering the restroom, and making eye contact with the man who's there.)

INT. STATION—PHILADELPHIA—NIGHT

RACHEL/SAMUEL

As the boy rouses himself, he says something to his mother. She nods . . .

He starts to go without his hat, but Rachel collars him and puts it on his head.

INT. MEN'S ROOM

It's a long row of sinks, urinals and stalls . . . (Samuel exchanges a look with a man washing his hands). Samuel proceeds along the row of doors, finally selects a stall near the end.

. . . Two other men have entered the men's room; one is a large BLACK MAN in a three-piece suit (McFee). His PARTNER (Fergie) is a caucasian in designer jeans and a short leather jacket.

FIRST TURNING POINT: (The first turning point of the scene is the attack, and the second act of this scene will focus on the murder.)

ACT TWO:

ANGLE IN SAMUEL'S STALL

They advance on the young man with unmistakeable menace . . . a savage, wordless struggle ensues . . .

BACK TO FIGHT

as the struggle builds to a climax . . . the black man motions for his partner to watch the door . . .

ANGLE IN SAMUEL'S STALL

as he edges open the stall door a crack. Over his shoulder . . . in the mirror . . . we catch a sight of the black man's face.

. . . the black man makes for the exit, then on second thought, glances at the row of stalls.

His P.O.V.—STALLS

All quiet, but . . .

SECOND TURNING POINT: (Here, Samuel makes a sound, which leads to the third act of the scene, where McFee checks the stalls, almost finding Samuel.)

ACT THREE:

The black man whips out a .357 magnum revolver and, starting at the near end, starts pushing open the stall doors.

. . . As the black man approaches, Samuel works desperately on the latch.

At the last minute, he finally wedges it in.

BLACK MAN

He elbows Samuel's stall . . . the door won't open.

ANGLE IN SAM'S STALL

Fighting back panic, Samuel has retreated as far as he can.

BLACK MAN

as he gives the door a kick. It holds . . .

In desperation, Samuel does the only thing he can think of . . . he slips under the partition into the neighboring stall that the black man just checked out. But he loses his hat in the process. His hand snakes back INTO FRAME to snatch it.

CLIMAX:

. . . just as the black man gives the door a ferocious kick that splinters the lock and nearly takes it off its hinges. He's framed there, the big muzzle of the .357 looking down our throats.

RESOLUTION:

A beat, then the black man holsters his weapon, and turns to follow his partner out.

CREATE A SEQUENCE OF SCENES

As you create scenes, think of their relationship to other scenes. The tighter the relationship between scenes, the clearer the flow and focus of the story (and the less the executive or producer can haphazardly change them around). Usually, there are several scenes that make up a sequence. The sequence might be the exciting chase scenes all around town that get shorter and shorter until finally the car crashes or the villain is caught. They might be the sequence of scenes that build to the final explosion (*The Guns of Navarone*) or the developing scenes that lead to the lovers finally reuniting (*When Harry Met Sally*) or the scenes that work against time as Mozart finally finishes his opera (*Amadeus*).

In *The Fugitive*, the first sequence of scenes might be "The Murder and The Sentencing," which take up the first eleven minutes of the film. They include the murder scene, the booking scene, and the trial scene. The next sequence might be called "The Escape," which leads through the train wreck. The next sequence could be called "After Him:" which includes the scenes of Deputy Sam Gerard starting the chase, leading up to Kimble arriving in Chicago. As you look at all the scenes in this film, you will notice that they are grouped together, each sequence relating to a certain idea and certain actions.

In all these sequences, a scene could not easily be removed without losing important beats. Every scene has a reason to be there. Every scene leads easily to the next scene. All of the information that we need is given to us before we need it. Deputy Gerard is clearly established as the U.S. Marshall <u>before</u> he begins questioning the guard. Kimble clearly gets the idea about going to Chicago to look for the one-armed man *before* setting out for the city.

LOOK AT THE RELATIONSHIP OF YOUR SCENES

The number of scenes you have in your script will vary. It may be 75 scenes, it may be 100 scenes. Some of your scenes may be very short establishing scenes—a Corridor, a Street, Inside a Car. Some will be more developed scenes of one-four pages. There is no correct number, although if you only have two or three scenes, you're not using the cinematic medium and are actually doing a play. If you have hundreds of scenes, the film will feel hurried, undeveloped, without adequate time to build the story.

As you look at your scenes, there are ways to get additional interest by looking at their relationships to each other.

CHOOSING SCENES FOR CONTRAST

Since film is about moving images, you can create strong images through the relationship of two scenes.

For instance, you might contrast a scene through the use of light and dark. The first scene is THE PARK—DAY. The next scene might be THE STREET—NIGHT.

Scenes might contrast through moods. An intimate, passionate lovemaking scene might contrast with an argument in the park. A violent scene might play off of a light, comedic scene. In *Fatal Attraction*, Alex and Dan are in bed together when Alex asks if he's up for something energetic. CUT TO: Dancing at a loud, frenzied club.

Scenes can contrast by varying long and short scenes, visual versus dialogue scenes, interior versus exterior scenes.

The pacing of the scenes can change from one to another, with a slow-paced scene of getting ready for bed followed by a car chase scene as the cop is called into action. In *The Fugitive*, there are a number of short reflective scenes when Gerard is once more on Kimble's trail.

97

Subject matter can be contrasted from scene to scene. You might move from a violent murder scene to a quiet scene inside a church. Or a family scene about an argument might contrast with another family scene that's peaceful and tranquil. (Many of Woody Allen's films have good contrasting scenes between different types of family relationships.)

Contrasting subject matter can be further enhanced through intercutting scenes. In *Schindler's List*, a wedding scene in the concentration camp is intercut with a scene of Schindler kissing a woman in the club, which is intercut with a scene of the Commandant beating Helen, the woman he has taken into his home. In *Cabaret*, there is also a similar scene as a beating outside in the alley is echoed with the music, noise, and laughter inside the cabaret. In *The Godfather*, a christening celebration is contrasted with a murder, in *The Godfather, Part II*, a parade intercuts with the murder, and in *The Godfather, Part III*, the opera scene is intercut with the murder scenes.

WHAT GOES WRONG WITH WELL-WRITTEN SCENES?

Scenes that work well do not exist in isolation but are part of a sequence that moves the story forward toward the climax. When films don't work well, often the problem lies with scenes that may be complete in themselves but are not connected to other scenes. This can be paricularly deadly in long films. If the scenes do not flow well, and are not well connected with the story spine and with each other, a two-hour film can feel like three hours. Compare your experience of watching the three-hour films of *Schindler's List, Dances with Wolves,* or *JFK* versus the experience of watching the long films of *The Last Emperor, Hope and Glory, The Incredible Lightness of Being,* and *Short Cuts.* These last four films have their own brilliance, but they feel long because many of the scenes are more static and descriptive rather than part of scene sequences that give the film momentum. When scenes stay on track, build, and have direction, the film involves you and moves you without consciousness of time.

Hope and Glory is a particularly good film to study to understand scene relationships. This is a charming, stylish, delightful work, but it is episodic without a strong driving force. Even though the individual scenes work beautifully, they don't combine to drive the story forward toward a clear climax. As a result, you don't have a sense of approaching the end of the film, and when the end comes, you may actually be a bit surprised because it seems arbitrary.

Sometimes scenes don't work because there is little momentum or dramatic build within the individual scene. Instead of building to make a particular point, the scene is flat, static, simply descriptive. The scenes might show a cop driving down the street, a woman writing in her journal, a man at work, and then the cop working in the office, the woman leaving for work, the man coming home. Although there's room in every film for some of these merely expositional or character scenes, if these overbalance the story scenes that move the story forward, the film will feel static. If you like the characters, you might be patient with the lack of build and drive to the story. If you don't like the characters, the ninty-minute film can feel like three hours.

To understand this concept, you may want to look at two small films that received a great deal of interest in 1993: *Ruby in Paradise* and *The Bad Lieutenant*. These new filmmakers clearly have talent and potential; nevertheless, many scenes are static, merely descriptive, and repetitious. You can see some of these same issues in films by Robert Altman and John Cassavetes. Although they are brilliant filmmakers on many levels, they generally lack strong story beats to pull their stories forward. If you love their characters and style (and, many times, I do), you can be patient with the episodic nature of the scenes. But remember that it is possible for a scene to function on many levels—strong character scenes and strong story scenes—while also exploring a theme and building an image.

APPLICATION

As you look at your scenes, ask yourself:

>Do all of my scenes have a reason for being in my story?

>Do the majority of my scenes move the story forward toward the climax?

>Have I structured most of my individual scenes so that they have a direction? A sense of going somewhere? A point to make?

>Is my entrance to the scene at the latest point, or am I giving information that isn't necessary before actually starting the scene?

>Do I get out of the scene after I've made the point rather than continuing to hang around, even though there's nothing more to be said?

>Have I remembered that scenes are about images? Have I remembered to play the image, to play the conflict, to play the emotions, rather than simply playing the information?

>Is the relationship of my scenes interesting? Are my scenes repetitive? flat? boring? or is there something exciting, dramatic, and fascinating happening?

>Will the audience be entertained—not just by the entire story, but by each individual scene, which builds to the climax?

Film creates a visual rhythm. It achieves its rhythm partly through the movement within the scenes, but also by the interplay of one scene with another. The contrasts, the build, the intensity, the character dynamics all work together to build the story through the scene.

If the scenes are working, you are well on your way to creating a script with momentum and clarity. Now you want to create a script that not only moves, but is also cohesive.

Chapter Six

Creating a Cohesive Script

Every art form strives for a sense of unity. Whether listen ing to a piece of music, looking at a painting, or watching a movie, we want to feel that it's all one piece, that it's cohesive. Different art forms attain cohesiveness in different ways. Music uses recurring musical motifs and rhythms. Sometimes a particular instrument threads its way throughout a symphony, playing the same melody. Sometimes the trombones, trumpets, or drums keep coming back to repeat a sound or rhythm. The music gains its sense of unity because we have a sense that it has a beginning, a middle, and an end, and the repetition lets us know that we are still in the same piece of music.

In art, a color or shape might repeat itself throughout a painting. In a patchwork quilt, the same type of material or the same shape may appear throughout. Architecture achieves cohesiveness from repeated patterns in windows and arches or with the use of light.

Film also needs a sense of unity and integration. Scripts gain cohesiveness through the use of foreshadowing and pay-off, recurring motifs, repetition, and contrast.

FORESHADOWING AND PAYOFF

All of us have watched murder mysteries in which the camera zooms in on a knife that is later used as the murder weapon, or in which a threat is made that is later carried out. These are the most obvious uses of **foreshadowing** and **payoff.** Foreshadowing is a visual clue or piece of dialogue that is used to set up an action, or a piece of information that is paid off at a later time in the story.

Usually we see foreshadowing and payoff in mysteries in which the audience often needs help in following the complex clues that lead to a solution. We might also see it in comedies, where jokes need to be set up to get the most laughter.

Near the beginning of the *Star Wars* trilogy, significant information is given about Luke Skywalker's father. This information is paid off when we discover that Darth Vader is his father. In *Tootsie*, we learn that occasionally a technical hitch happens to the tape, and the show has to go live. This information is paid off when Michael sees his opportunity to unmask at the climax of the film.

Most films use some sort of foreshadowing and payoff. In *The African Queen*, Charlie explains about the fort they'll have to pass before torpedoing the *Louisa*, foreshadowing the danger that they'll experience as they go down the river.

> ALLNUTT
> If there's any place along the whole river the Germans'll keep a lookout, it'll be Shona. 'Cause that's where the old road ferries over from the south.

> ROSE
> But they can't do anything to us!

> ALLNUTT
> Oh they can't, eh? They got rifles, maybe ma-

chine guns, maybe even cannons, and just one bullet in that blastin' gelatin an', Miss. what's left of us would be in bits and pieces.

ROSE

Then we'll go by night.

ALLNUTT

Oh no we won't.

ROSE

Now why not?

ALLNUTT

Cause the rapids start just a little ways below Shona, an' they ain't nobody in his right mind'ud tackle 'em even in daylight, let alone at night.

ROSE

Then we'll go in daylight. We'll go on the far side of the river from Shona, just as fast as ever we can.

They do go, and everything is just like they said it would be.

Here we see foreshadowing and payoff used in a fairly straightforward way. The dialogue indicates that something will happen, and later it happens.

In *Gone With the Wind*, Rhett Butler tells Scarlett, as they leave the burning city of Atlanta, that she's looking at the dying of the old South. And the film proves that Rhett's words are correct.

In *Back to the Future*, we see some unusual cases of foreshadowing and payoff. This very tight script is probably one of the best examples of ways to use foreshadowing and payoff are used to achieve unity, humor, and tension in the story.

Creating the relationship between present and past took very careful writing. Much of the humor and sense of story unity came from this attention to detail.

There are several types of foreshadowing and payoff in *Back to the Future*. The first type of foreshadowing is informative. It sets up what will happen and what to expect. Much of this revolves around how the time machine and time travel operate. Professor Brown explains:

> BROWN
> Welcome to my latest experiment. This is the big one—the one I've been waiting for all my life . . . If my calculations are correct, when this car hits 88 miles an hour, you're gonna see some serious shit.

And it works just as he says it will. At 88 miles per hour, Marty is speeded into the past. Brown explains the Flux Capacitor, the clock, and the type of fuel used, which causes all sorts of complications later on.

> MARTY
> Does it run on unleaded gasoline?

> BROWN
> Unfortunately, no. It requires something with a little more kick . . .

Brown indicates a container with purple radioactivity symbols on it. Plutonium!

> MARTY
> Plutonium?

Later, there's not enough plutonium to get Marty back to the future and Brown begins to despair as he realizes how much power is needed to make the time machine work.

> BROWN
> 1.21 jiggowatts. How am I going to generate that
> kind of power? . . . The only power source ca-
> pable of triggering that kind of energy is a bolt
> of lightning . . . Unfortunately, you never know
> when or where lightning is going to strike.

This leads us to the second type of foreshadowing, in which an object or information is set up in one context and paid off in another. This kind of foreshadowing is subtle and pays off with surprise and unpredictability. It works by first giving us some information that seems unimportant, but later pays off as we begin to understand its significance. In *Back to the Future*, notice how the important information about the clock tower is presented.

At the beginning of the film, while Marty and Jennifer are discussing their plans to get together for a weekend, a "clock tower activist" gives them a flier, screaming, "Save the clock tower! Save the clock tower!" The flier mentions the date—and the time—that the clock stopped ticking when it was hit by lightning years ago. Jennifer takes the flier, but changes its function. Instead of focusing on the information about the clock tower, she uses it to write down her phone number and a message to Marty: "I love you!" Later, in the past, when Marty mentions why it's so urgent that he return to the future, he uses Jennifer's loving message as the reason.

> MARTY
> But I can't be stuck here. Don't you understand,
> Doc? I have a life in 1985! I've gotta get back!
> My girl friend's waiting for me . . . See what
> she wrote here?

And he pulls out the clock-tower flier.
And then, as Marty turns over the flier, he notices that there is a way to know when lightning will strike. There is a way to

harness the energy that will return him back to the future. The clock-tower flier gives specific information about where—and when—lightning will strike.

Just as an object can foreshadow and pay off important information, dialogue can also be used to plant some information that seems irrelevant in one context and highly important in another.

For instance, in 1985, Professor Brown mentions the historic date of November 5, 1955:

> BROWN
> That was the day I invented time travel . . . I was standing on the edge of my toilet, hanging a clock . . . I slipped and hit my head on the sink and when I came to, I had a revelation . . . a vision . . . It's taken me almost thirty years and my entire family fortune to fulfill the vision of that day.

Later, when Marty arrives at Dr. Brown's door in 1955 with an incredible tale about Brown's new time-travel machine of 1985, he notices the Band-Aid on Brown's forehead and convinces the doctor that he's telling the truth about knowing him in 1985.

> MARTY
> Dr. Brown . . . That bruise on your head. I know how you got it! It happened this morning! You fell off your toilet and hit your head on the sink! And then you came up with the idea of the Flux Capacitor, which is the heart of the time machine!

Much of the information about the relationship between George and Lorraine is presented in a similar way, as a sidelight in the present that becomes a motivating force for Marty in the past. In Act One, Lorraine mentions how she and George first met when her father hit George with his car.

She goes on to explain their first date:

> LORRAINE
>
> I'll never forget it . . . It was the night of that
> terrible thunderstorm . . . Your father *kissed* me
> for the first time on the dance floor—and that
> was when I realized I was going to spend the
> rest of my life with him.

Since the kiss set up the marriage, without the kiss, there would be no marriage—and no Marty. It becomes essential for Marty to bring his parents together to save his own life. The seriousness of this condition is further foreshadowed by Professor Brown, who realizes the effect that Marty could have on future events.

> BROWN
>
> You must stay in this house. Anything you do
> could have serious repercussions on future
> events . . . Marty, who else did you interact
> with today? Besides me?

> MARTY
>
> Well, nobody really. I just sort of bumped into
> my parents . . .

> BROWN
>
> You interfered with your parents' first meeting
> . . . All right, kid. You stick to your pop like
> glue, and make sure he takes her to the dance.

Sometimes foreshadowing and payoff are used for humor, to give a sense of integration to the script without necessarily being essential to the story. For instance, in 1985, we see the campaign to elect Goldie Wilson as mayor. In 1955, we see how Marty planted the "political" idea in Wilson's mind.

> WILSON
> I'm gonna make something of myself.

> MARTY
> That's right, he's gonna be Mayor someday.

> WILSON
> Mayor . . . That's a good idea! I could run for
> Mayor!

Lorraine's brother Joey is foreshadowed in Act One, and paid off—with humor—in Act Two. In the present, Lorraine has prepared a cake, hoping to welcome her brother home from prison. Unfortunately, poor Joey didn't make parole again. In the past we learn why.

> LORRAINE'S MOTHER
> Little Joey loves being in his pen. He actually
> cries when we take him out, so we leave him
> in there all the time . . . it seems to make him
> happy.

Even the seemingly unimportant information that the young George liked to write science-fiction stories gets paid off in the resolution when we see that he's just published his first book.

Notice, in all these examples, that nothing is forgotten, nothing is dropped. Every element that is set up and foreshadowed gets paid off somewhere else in the script. Whatever is needed to make the story work at the end is planted somewhere in the beginning.

RECURRING MOTIFS

Whereas foreshadowing and payoff usually relate to the story, motifs tend to be more thematic. A **motif** is a recurring image or rhythm or sound that is used throughout the film to deepen and dimensionalize the storyline and add texture to the theme. Motifs need at least three beats—or repetitions—to work. When they work best, they continue throughout the entire film, helping the audience to focus on certain elements.

One of the most recognizable motifs in any film is actually one of sound—the sound of *Jaws*. Whenever the shark comes near, we hear the dum-dum-dum-dum sound. This sound is set up immediately, in the first three minutes of the film, and is used each time the shark comes near, except for one time— when the shark makes its first attack on Quint, Matt, and Martin. Tension is gained each time by anticipation. We expect the shark to strike again. The one time the sound motif is not used, the scare is even greater because it's unexpected.

In *Ghostbusters*, we see the recurring motif of the lions, which later become the dogs of Zul. This image continues to appear in various guises: as the lions at the library, the terrible dog in Dana's refridgerator, and, eventually, the terror dogs that possess Dana and Louis. Each time we see these images, they change, becoming more sinister. Eventually they break apart, releasing Dana and Louis from their possession and allowing New York's citizens to go on to live another fun-filled day.

In *Cocoon*, we see a motif that is even less connected to the story, but that nevertheless adds dimension and texture to the film—the dolphin. At the beginning of the film, clouds form and something strange happens in the sky while dolphins respond in the sea. Later, dolphins are nearby as the centuries-old cocoons are removed from the water. Dolphins are nearby again when the cocoons are returned to the sea in Act Three.

These animals are used metaphorically in the film. Their image relies on our many associations with this sea creature, which seems the most "human" of all sea animals. They have their own language and are known to be gentle and peaceful animals. Surrounding the Anterians with dolphins gives us a subliminal association between two unlike species, since they have similar qualities. As a result, we see them as friendly aliens, as peaceful, and as worthy of our help. This motif dimensionalizes the Anterians and gives us clues about how we're to think and feel about their mission.

Witness gains cohesiveness through a recurring grain motif. The changes in the use of grain throughout the film symbolize changes that both John Book and the community undergo throughout the film. These grain images either reinforce the simplicity and gentleness of this community or gain added dramatic power through contrast. At the beginning, we see the Amish walking through the grain to a funeral. They are a farming community that live in harmony with the earth, as shown by the image of them emerging from the tall grain as they walk to the house. During the funeral scene, bread is placed on the table. Here the grain has been transformed, but it remains natural, wholesome, nurturing. In the city, Rachel and John Book break bread together by eating a hot dog and bun at a fast-food restaurant. Here the grain has been corrupted, processed, changed from its normal, healthy, natural state, just as Rachel and Samuel have been corrupted by the city. In Act Two, Rachel hides the bullets in the flour, showing that violence and harmony are now integrally connected through John's presence in this community. And in Act Three, the grain in the silo becomes a weapon of death. It is the ultimate symbol of the violence that has come to this peaceful community.

REPETITION AND CONTRAST

Anything that repeats an idea or image in a script can be seen as a repetition. A repetition can come through images, through dialogue, through character traits, through sound, or through the use of all these combined to keep the audience focused on an idea.

For instance, if you were doing a story about an alcoholic man, you might repeat that information about your character in a variety of ways. You might first show him drinking. Later, you might show him sleeping it off. Another time he might be in a house filled with empty wine bottles. In other scenes, you might show him staggering down a street, or fishing for money to buy beer, or in despair as a result of his drinking. Using a variety of images and characteristics, you would keep the audience focused by threading this information throughout the script.

Just as repetition helps to keep the script focused, so does the use of contrast, since it depends on us remembering something in the past that will be contrasted in the future. Because we've learned about the Amish way of nonviolence, John Book's response at the end of Act Three shocks the tourists when he punches the punks in a decidedly non-Amish way.

In *Gone With the Wind*, the first and second parts of the film contrast the kind of living that has gone with the wind. We see the contrasts of Four Oaks—before and after; Tara—before and after; of Mr. O'Hara—before and after; and the changes in Scarlett—before and after the war.

Back to the Future uses contrasts for humor—from the Ronald Reagan film in the 1950s, to the different type of skateboards used in the present and the past, to the changes in Biff, George, and Lorraine—before and after.

Contrasts allow the writer to play opposites and to help the audience make connections by showing the differences between one part of the story and another. A contrast throws certain information into high relief, making us notice it more because we've been introduced to its opposite.

You can use contrasts to show the differences in characters, scenes, locations, textures, and energy. You might contrast characters—perhaps pairing up two vastly different kinds of people, such as Eddie Murphy and Nick Nolte in *48 Hours*, or contrasting brunette Beth (the wife) and blonde Alex (the mistress) in *Fatal Attraction.*

Jaws contrasts the frivolity and fun of a beach party with the death of a swimmer moments later. *Witness* contrasts the textures, noise, and frenetic energy of the city with the slower country life of the Amish in Act Two. And *The African Queen* contrasts two very unlike characters—Rose and Allnutt—as they share a common goal.

Contrasts, repetitions, motifs, foreshadowing, and payoffs are all ways of giving unity to a story, of tightening the thematic line, and of keeping the audience focused where you want its focus to be.

PROBLEMS IN UNIFYING A SCRIPT

The process of rewriting often works against creating a unified script. Many rewrite discussions center on sections of the script, rather than the script as a whole. Perhaps a director wants to rework the murder scene, not realizing that changing the pay-off demands finding a whole new approach to foreshadowing in an earlier scene. Once, I arrived at a meeting that began with the writer-director and producer informing me that they decided to add a murder in the first scene. They didn't realize that it would change the storyline from then on. After twelve hours of trying to make it work without losing the excellent scenes that followed, we decided not to do it.

Problems in unifying a script are particularly prevalent in mystery and espionage stories. Some executives refuse to buy these scripts, believing that the public isn't interested since they generally don't do well at the box office. Actually, many of us love a good puzzle, but few are satisfying because clues are dropped out, or information isn't set up and paid off in ways that keep us with the story. Think about *Gorky Park, The Little Drummer Girl*, and *The Osterman Weekend*, all of which did less-than-satisfactory business. In spite of some exciting action and intriguing storylines, all of these movies had problems with clarity of information. Insufficient foreshadowing and payoff contributed to their lack of success.

Dramas, comedies, Westerns, and science-fiction films also need clarity in the way they present information. *The Mission* received some criticism for unclear set-up and payoff regarding its geography. Sometimes it was difficult to get up the mountain, sometimes it was relatively easy. The unity between the foreshadowing of the difficulty in Act One and the payoff during the battle scenes in Act Three didn't always mesh.

The same criticism was given for *Full Metal Jacket* and *No Way Out*. Some critics felt that *The Color of Money* was essentially two different films since some of the twists at the end did not connect with the set-up at the beginning. And we've all seen innumerable detective stories and mysteries that lost us somewhere along the way because the script didn't quite fit together.

Unifying the script is one of the most difficult jobs of the rewrite. As these examples show, even brilliant filmmakers sometimes fall short of creating a cohesive script. It demands great attention to detail, a thorough analysis, and constant attention to the script as a whole. But there are innumerable payoffs for this attention—in critical and box-office success and Academy Awards.

APPLICATION

The rewriting process is the best time to begin to build up and weave these elements into the script. Many times a writer doesn't know that she has the beginning of a motif in a script, or that something that is paid off can be further foreshadowed for greater dramatic punch and unity. Working with these elements demands doing a thorough check of how they are working in your story.

When you begin rewriting, it will be helpful first to make sure that everything you've foreshadowed is paid off and everything that's paid off is foreshadowed. If you've already done several rewrites, you may discover that some foreshadowing might have been dropped from the script as you moved from one rewrite to the next. Or what you thought was paid off never was—except in your mind's eye. So carefully follow through every thread, or the script will have loose ends.

Look for motifs that can be expanded. To do this, you might find it helpful to look through the physical objects you've used in the script. Could any of these be expanded upon to create a recurring-image motif? Or there might be some sound that's an integral part of your story that needs to be created as a motif. In a mystery, it could be the sound of squeaky shoes that might work as both a motif and as foreshadowing and payoff. In a space story, it might be a recurring rhythm, such as the sound used in *Close Encounters of the Third Kind* to communicate with the aliens. Then ask yourself:

Is everything I've paid off foreshadowed in the script? Is everything I've foreshadowed paid off in the script?

Have I found original ways to foreshadow and pay off information? Have I changed functions, or disguised foreshadowing information, or used humor to set up and pay off information?

Have I created or implied motifs that the director could use to integrate the script visually? Have I thought through my script visually, repeating images that will give it a sense of cohesiveness?

Have I contrasted scenes, characters, actions, even images to give my script more dramatic texture and punch?

Have I done at least one rewrite during which I tried to see the script as a whole, rather than focus on the individual parts?

Part of the joy of rewriting is the opportunity to draw out these relationships. It's a chance to expand on themes and images by threading them throughout the script. But in order to find potential images that can dimensionalize the story and theme, it becomes necessary to explore the thematic lines of a script, to ask yourself, "What does it really mean and how can I build meanings dramatically through images?" Part Two will begin the exploration of how to clarify and execute the theme behind the story.

Part Two

Idea Development

Chapter Seven

Making It Commercial

No matter how good a writer you are, and no matter how good your script is, there will still be one question asked by all producers and executives: "Is it commercial?"

Everyone has different ideas about what "commercial" is. Many producers think that it's a matter of packaging. "Get the right actors, and it will be commercial." Many of them say, "If we can only get Meryl Streep, or Tom Cruise, or Robert Redford, or Barbra Streisand, then it'll be commercial." However, every one of these people has had box-office failures.

Some people think that commercial depends on the subject matter. They look for trends and try to capitalize on what's the "in" subject. *Platoon* seemed to imply that Vietnam movies were "in." But *The Hanoi Hilton* disproved that theory. After *War Games*, computer films seemed a good bet. But *D.A.R.Y.L.* came and went with little box-office business. After *Star Wars*, space movies seemed like the thing to do, but *The Black Hole* and *Ice Pirates* showed that that was not the case.

Some people think that the answer is to look for an exciting, best-selling novel to make into a film. That would seem to be true, but *Raise the Titanic* was partially responsible for the demise of Marble Arch Productions, *Bonfire of the Vanities* was a box-office disaster, and even films based on exciting books, such as *Coma* and *The Little Drummer Girl*, did only so-so business.

Well, what about doing sequels? *Rocky I, Rocky II, Rocky III,* and *Rocky IV* seem to point toward built-in success. But what about *Jaws 3-D*? Furthermore, sequels can be very difficult to write. *Rambo* came out years after *First Blood*, and it took seventeen rewrites before it had a workable storyline. Rarely do sequels do as well as the first film. Generally, the sequel lacks the charm, or clarity or originality, of the first film. Think of such sequels as *Ghostbusters II, Look Who's Talking II,* or *Jaws 3-D*.

For every neat theory about commercial success, there seem to be examples that disprove the point. However, there are certain elements we can discuss that seem to contribute decisively to the success of a film and that are not dependent on the writer's close personal friendship with Meryl Streep or Robert Redford.

THE THREE ELEMENTS NECESSARY FOR SUCCESS

One way of thinking about commercial success is to remember that it is never dependent on any one element. We might look at the elements that help make a successful script as: (1) marketability, (2) creativity, and (3) script structure. If any one of these is missing, there's a good chance that the script will not sell, and that even if it does sell, it won't do well at the box office.

We discussed story structure in the first six chapters. If a story isn't tight, if it doesn't make sense, it will have a difficult time in any kind of market. Certainly we've all seen films that were sold and then produced without having a solid story structure—a few of these even did well at the box office. But these exceptions are very rare. Most of the big box-office successes, such as *Star Wars, Back to the Future, Jaws, Raiders of the Lost*

Ark, E.T., and *Ghostbusters,* have well-structured stories. Good structure has been proven over and over again as an essential ingredient to a film's success—in spite of all the "right" commercial ingredients.

Structure, by itself, means little without creative writers. When producers talk about creativity, they usually mean: "Is it fresh? Is it original? Is it different? Is it unique?" They can also mean: "Does it have a hook? Is it compelling? Am I grabbed by the premise?" Many of the most successful commercial films are based on an original premise that is well executed. There were no precedents for films such as *Ghostbusters, WarGames, Ruthless People,* and *E.T.,* and there have been no successful copies. So without something very special that's upheld by good writing, it will be difficult to make a good script great!

But creativity, by itself, will still not make the sale. There need to be elements that can help market the script and that also capture the audiences.

Marketability might be thought of as those elements that make people want to invest in a film and that make it *look* like it has a reasonable chance of success. Certainly, casting Robert Redford and Meryl Streep in *Out of Africa* was a very smart choice. Although Sidney Pollock had wanted to do this book for years, the particular choice of actors made it possible. Marketability can also mean other packaging choices. A script directed by Peter Weir, Barry Levinson, or Oliver Stone has a better chance of being made than one directed by an unknown, first-time director. A film produced by Ed Feldman or Saul Zaentz or Richard Zanuck already has an important element in its favor.

But marketability and salability are not limited to just packaging the project, and they need not be amorphous words based on the whim of an executive. There are some commercial elements that can be defined and explained because there are underlying concepts that make people want to go see a movie. These elements can be developed and focused in your script to make it more commercial.

119

Generally, people go to films because there is something within the film that speaks to them. They identify in some way with both the characters and the story. They connect. "Connections" is the key word for marketability. There are specific ways that people connect to a film and understanding them can help you bring out the commercial elements in your script.

HOW TO FIND THE CONNECTIONS

Universal Appeal of the Idea

Most films that are dramatically successful express some underlying idea that has universal appeal for audiences. There's something beneath the story that captures the audience and speaks to it. This idea causes audiences to identify with the characters and situations, usually because the theme tells us something about our human condition. Ideas convey the meaning of events—what the writer believes about why things happen, what we can learn from them, about cause and effect and the meaning of life. The idea might be about the meaning of something we've experienced (if you're reckless in sex, you can jeopardize your family [*Fatal Attraction*], or violence has far-reaching effects on the lives of those who practice it [*Unforgiven*], or about an underlying message that the writer wants to communicate through a story rather than through an essay (perhaps that common decency combined with opportunity can lead to an "Absolute Good" as in *Schindler's List*).

Many times this idea can be expressed very simply. One of the most prevalent ideas in many successful films is "underdog triumphs." Think of the number of "underdog triumphs" films that have done well: *Rocky, The Karate Kid, Ghostbusters,* and *Places in the Heart*. This idea is very workable because all of us want to overcome adverse circumstances. By watching the success of the underdog on the screen, we're able to triumph vicariously.

"Revenge" is another theme that has universal significance. Have you ever felt like getting back at someone? Dirty Harry can do it for you. Or Charles Bronson. Ever feel angry at competition in the area of romance? *Medea* will carry out revenge, and we identify because, on some level, we've all been betrayed. Did you feel betrayed and angry by our ambivalent attitude toward the Vietnam War? Rambo will make it simple—and take care of all the bad guys who robbed us of victory.

Another common theme that helps us identify with the story is "triumph of the human spirit." This theme was used very successfully in such films as *Places in the Heart* and *The Color Purple*, and with the Emmy Award winners *Do You Remember Love?* and *Love is Never Silent*.

Why do we watch all those films about rich people outsmarting other rich people to get richer? Because greed is an understandable feeling. We've all felt it at some time, along with envy, jealousy, and the more socially acceptable emotion, the desire to "have it all."

Some themes seem particularly relevant to certain age groups. If you know the demographics of your audience, you can capitalize on universal themes that will appeal to them. For instance, about sixty percent of moviegoers are between the age of thirteen and thirty. That's why many "coming of age" and "identity" stories, such as *Risky Business, Porky's, The Breakfast Club,* and *Stand by Me,* have made such successful movies. Even a film like *The Big Chill,* which seems like it shouldn't have been commercial at all, spoke to many of us because it had to do with our experiences and our identity at a certain point in time.

Other experiences are less accessible to everyone, but nevertheless they can make connections with audience members. These include themes like "integrity," as in *A Man for All Seasons*, or "resolution and completion," as in *The Trip to Bountiful* or *On Golden Pond,* or "redemption," perhaps by a person saving or redeeming their reputation, as in *Absence of Malice* or *The Verdict*.

You can see that all of these themes have to do with psychological and emotional states, or life processes such as "coming of age" and "finding one's identity." Many good writers are well-versed in human psychology. They observe. They read. They interpret. They study the human animal in order to figure out what it does and why it does it. The more descriptive they can be, the more accurately they can portray us, the more likely we are to want to watch their characters on the screen.

Finding Commercial Aspects through Trends

Most successful films have one underlying universal theme that connects with the audience. Many of these films, however, also connect because the timing is perfect. Remember *The China Syndrome*, which premiered the same week as the Three Mile Island disaster? The nuclear accident actually helped the success of the film. *The Big Chill* came out just as those who had lived through the sixties were old enough to experience some nostalgia for those other times. *WarGames* premiered at about the same time that there were numerous news stories about kids who had tapped into computers. And many of the films by Sylvester Stallone echoed the more conservative political climate of the 1980s.

Since films take several years to sell, make, and release, it seems miraculous that any movie can capture a social trend. To understand how this might happen, think of the work of the artist. Artists have always tended to be ahead of their times. They understand currents and trends in the beginning stages, and they find a voice and an expression for movements that might still be locked in the subconscious of the rest of the population.

Beginning in the early 1980s, there was an emphasis on the nuclear family, both in politics and in television sitcoms. (Think of "The Cosby Show," "Family Ties," "The Jeffersons," "Growing Pains," and, later, "Roseanne" and "Married . . . With Children" which are variations on the same idea). Since the mid-1980s as more and more baby-boomers had children while also gaining positions of power in the film industry, we saw more films about children (remember *Baby Boom, Look Who's Talking, For Keeps, Three Men and a Baby, Raising Arizona, She's Having a Baby, Kindergarten Cop,* or the more recent *Mrs. Doubtfire).* In the 1990s, new themes are emerging in both politics and entertainment—ecology (the film about Chico Mendes should be in theatres in late 1994 or 1995), a message about non-violence (*Unforgiven*), the difficulties of the twentysomethings (*Reality Bites*), the issues that confront the fortysomethings living in a big city (*Grand Canyon*), or the desire to heal old wounds that have been part of the lives of baby-boomers as well as the national consciousness (*Heaven and Earth*).

Most successful films, which depend in some way on trends and topicality, capitalize on commercial connections by also emphasizing the personal side of the story.

MAKING IT PERSONAL

The personal side of finding connections is made up of two elements, the descriptive and the prescriptive. The descriptive tells us "how it is." The prescriptive describes "how we'd like it to be." A film can capitalize on either—or both—of these elements to achieve success.

Descriptive writing accurately and realistically shows how a certain type of character will act and react within a particular situation. We've all seen films where the reactions seem so "true." Perhaps it's *Porky's,* during which audiences say, "That's just how those guys would act," or *Stand by Me,* with its honest portrayal of a group of twelve-year-olds and their uncertainties and fears.

In many television movies, success depends on getting the characters and emotions just right. When watching television movies like *The Burning Bed, Do You Remember Love?, Heartsounds, M.A.D.D.,* or *Adam,* we notice how everything rings true. These movies have described people accurately, and they have achieved success because they echo the experiences of audiences.

Prescriptive films show us our ideals. Many of these films are "hero" films. The hero rarely feels fear, or uncertainty, or lack of confidence (which all of us would probably feel in that same situation). Instead, the hero acts out how we would like to be. As a result, we live vicariously through the hero, all the while knowing it's not really real.

Descriptive and prescriptive elements can be defined in three different ways: the physical, the psychological, and the emotional. In working with specific characters, it's possible to deepen the descriptive dimensions by "physicalizing" your character and asking yourself, "What would my character really look like in this situation?" If he's a fifteen-year-old boy in love for the first time, he might blush, he might be awkward, he might wear glasses, he might try an "in" hairstyle that doesn't quite work. Psychologically, he might lack confidence, or he might try to imitate the football hero because he's unsure of his own good qualities. Emotionally, he might get angry and irritable, or want to be left alone, or even laugh too much.

If you're doing a prescriptive film, your character might be the class leader or the football hero. Physically, he'd probably be strong, tall, and good-looking, the kind of guy who always looks terrific no matter what he wears. Psychologically, he'd probably be very confident, not have a care in the world, and believe that he can do anything he sets out to do. Emotionally, he's probably steady as a rock, impervious to pain and fear, and nothing fazes him.

Many films connect to the audiences on both of these levels, either creating some descriptive and some prescriptive characters, or creating a transformational arc for the main character that moves from the descriptive to the prescriptive, from uncertainty to the heroic *(Rocky, Karate Kid)*. This is another reason why the "underdog triumphs" films are so popular. Not only do they have a universal and understandable theme, but they connect us to the character's personal transformation.

Connecting through the Stakes

It's not unusual to hear a producer or executive ask a writer, "But what's at stake?" If the jeopardy is unclear, if there's not a reason to care about the character, then the audience is unable to see any connections between their experience and the experience of the character.

Stakes can sometimes be thought of as what we need to do to survive in our world. Certainly, we need to have enough to eat and drink, to have a roof over our heads, and to be safe. Many films put these basic needs in jeopardy in order to raise the level of identification and concern of the audience. But there are many other stakes to play, and audiences can connect at many different levels.

Noted psychologist Abraham Maslowe devised a seven-part hierarchy of human needs that explains and clarifies what drives us, what we want, and what's at stake if we don't get it. Many successful films have spoken directly to these needs. Any one of these seven psychological stakes can be in jeopardy at various times in a film, and most good films will draw on more than one of them.

1. Survival. Many good films are about survival. It's a basic instinct and common to all animals. We want to survive, and we will go to considerable lengths to do so. Many action-adventures are successful because we all identify with the life-against-death situations they present. *Deliverance* has considerable power because of the life-and-death stakes. James Bond is constantly in life-and-death situations. Many hijacking and women-in-jeopardy films are successful because we identify with the basic life-and-death situation. A great deal of drama speaks to survival needs because it is the one basic drive that we can all understand. Films that speak to this need also work well because they are essentially dramatic. The conflict is always clear, there's always plenty of action and momentum, and they involve us and bring ultimate identification to the situation.

2. Safety and Security. Once basic survival needs are taken care of, people need to feel that they are in a place that is safe, secure, and protective. We might call this a place to call home or a safe haven. We lock our doors at night, forts are built for protection, armies stand guard—so that we can feel safe. Many films, such as *Places in the Heart, Country,* and *Voyage of the Damned*, have dealt with the search for safety and security. The same can be said of the film and long-running TV series *The Fugitive,* as well as innumerable Westerns in which pioneers search for a protective haven.

3. Love and Belonging. Once people have a home, it's natural to desire a sense of family. This can be a yearning for a nuclear family or for a sense of community. People need to connect, and this need is answered in many films in many different ways. In *Places of the Heart*, Edna wants to preserve her family, but her family includes more than just her children. It includes Moses, the black man; Will, the blind man; and the town she's lived in for so long. In *Back to the Future*, along with Marty's survival, the family is also at stake. Many films, such as *Porky's,* the *Police Academy* films, *My Fair Lady*, and even *Witness*, deal with acceptance into a group. Some films deal with the search for the perfect mate, or the need to belong to someone. Some films deal with the creation of the family and the need for warmth, acceptance, and love. We find this in many successful sitcoms, such as "Family Ties," "The Cosby Show," "Little House on the Prairie," and even "All in the Family."

4. Esteem and Self-Respect. Whereas the need for love and belonging often deal with unconditional acceptance, self-esteem and self-respect are earned. People want to be looked up to and be recognized for their skills and contributions. Many times, this means that the group accepts you because of what you've done. This can be the respect that Luke Skywalker earned at the end of *Star Wars*, or the various rewards that James Bond receives after successfully completing a mission, or the confidence that Celie achieves at the end of *The Color Purple*. Many stories about integrity, such as *Gandhi* or *Martin Luther King, Jr.*, deal with this need, as well as television's "Afterschool Specials," in which the story might be about winning an award, successfully completing a science project, or being accepted as a member of the team. Movies-of-the-Week, such as *The $5.20-an-Hour Dream,* also address this need of overcoming discrimination and the desire for achievement and recognition.

5. The Need to Know and Understand. We are born curious. We have a natural desire to know how things work, to understand how things fit together. We like to figure things out, to search for the knowledge that makes it possible for us to do many wonderful things. Think of the many time-travel films, such as *Back to the Future, Time After Time,* or *The Time Machine*, that show someone trying to figure out how to travel in time. Many films about scientists (mad or otherwise) deal with this need, such as *Frankenstein* and *Madame Curie*. Detective films capture us, echoing our own need to get answers. *Chinatown, The Maltese Falcon,* and *North by Northwest* all involve us in this basic search.

6. The Aesthetic. People who are secure, confident, and experience love have a need for balance, a sense of order in life, a sense of being connected with something greater than themselves. This can be thought of as a spiritual or aesthetic need that sometimes drives people to a religious experience (*Song of Bernadette, Joan of Arc*), or an experience with nature (*Never Cry Wolf*), or even the combination of religious and artistic experiences, as in the award-winning *Amadeus*. This particular need is often difficult to convey since it's the most abstract and perhaps the least universal. However, it is a recognizable need, and films that can make it tangible and understandable can do well at the box office.

7. Self-Actualization. All of us need to express ourselves to communicate who we are, to actualize our talents, skills, and abilities. Writers certainly can understand this, and many films about struggling writers, composers, and athletes have been successful because we root for these people to succeed. Self-actualization needs go a step further, because they pertain to self-expression, whether or not one is publically recognized or rewarded. It's one thing to paint in hopes of becoming famous or winning an award; it's quite another thing to paint because we *have* to, and we do it regardless of any recognition.

Self-actualization needs can pertain to artists or athletes, but also to personality needs. A comedian *has* to be funny, a doctor *has* to heal, an aviator *has* to fly. These people come alive when they are doing what they have to do. And that drive, when we see it in a film, is always worth rooting for. Think of the number of films that express this drive: the need to dance in *The Turning Point*, Kimberly's desire to use her reporting talent in *The China Syndrome*, and the need to run in *Chariots of Fire*.

Raising the Stakes   To raise the stakes in any film, you can work with these needs in a variety of ways. You can raise the stakes by including more than one stake in any film. Notice how *Places in the Heart* deals with the needs for safety and security, survival, love and belonging, and self-actualization. *Witness* works with the needs for survival, love and belonging, and esteem and self-respect. *The African Queen* has survival at stake, as well as safety and security, love and belonging, and self-actualization. The more stakes you can play in a film, the more opportunity you have for hooking the audience and giving them something universal to connect with in your story.

You can also raise the stakes throughout the story by keeping the goal out of reach and making it look throughout the story as if the character will not achieve the goal. A real, workable goal is never easy to achieve. If we identify with the need, but also are concerned that the character will not achieve it, we vicariously live through the character's journey, causing further emotional connections.

The more we experience the character's desire to achieve the goal, the more we can connect with the character. This means raising the stakes by playing the emotions that are connected with any journey toward achieving one's needs. There are many emotions that come into play in this search: anger, fear, joy, uncertainty, despair, and hope. The more emotional range you give your characters in their search, the more understandable the characters will be. Many films *only* show the action necessary to achieve the goal. As a result, the audience will feel distanced from the characters, and it will be difficult for them to identify with the stakes. By playing emotions as well as the action, the stakes seem larger because we are better able to identify with them.

As you move up the scale of needs, the kind of film you do will change. Survival needs usually demand an action-oriented film. These needs are basic to action-adventure films, disaster films, horror films, and most Westerns. Belonging and self-expression needs usually contain more emotional content. They tend to be more relational, less hard-edged, and often contain humor and warmth. Aesthetic needs or the need to know usually will rely more on the philosophical side of the character. It will be more thematic, perhaps "talkier," and seemingly more abstract. Characters in these films think, ponder, and figure out, which can sometimes create a boring, talky film. However, in the right hands, this can be an intelligent, fascinating story.

COMMUNICATING THE THEME

Once you know what to say, you also need to know how to say it. Theme is the least interesting when it's communicated through talky dialogue, when it's said rather than expressed through more dramatic means. Although lines of dialogue here and there can express the theme (re-watch *Room with a View* to see how dialogue can express the theme of identity without getting talky), the theme will be far better expressed by concentrating on other more cinematic choices.

Writers can communicate theme through the story choices

that they make. Events have meaning, and they communicate what you believe about why things happen in life. Deciding that a character gets robbed and mugged because they happen to be in the wrong place at the wrong time can communicate your idea that life is haphazard and nonsensical. Choosing characters that respond compassionately to each other can communicate that you believe that the world is a loving and caring place. Showing characters whose lives continually meet and intersect may communicate your idea about fate and destiny.

Theme can be communicated through decisions that your characters make within the story. The fact that your character chooses to fight the bad guy can show courage or integrity or a sense of justice. The character that makes a decision to change during the story shows themes of transformation and growth. Themes of corruption, greed, cowardice and disillusionment can easily be expressed dramatically through character actions.

One of the most important methods for communicating theme focuses on the images chosen by the writer, and later by the director. Since film is a visual medium, the images that you create can give many levels of meaning to your story. You might use images of light and dark to show good and evil, or small versus large spaces to show oppression versus freedom. In *Deliverance,* images of civilization and land development contrast with images of the primitive, communicating a theme about the rawness that these men encounter in the wilderness. *Taxi Driver* uses images of the dark and gritty city to communicate its view of life. *Body Heat* uses images of heat and fire to communicate passions out of control. *Fatal Attraction* places Alex in a loft apartment in the middle of a meat-packing hellhole in the city. Her apartment is a labyrinth of rooms and columns, imaging the shadowy, non-direct qualities that make up the character of Alex. In *The Fugitive*, images of the city as an immense grid show how easy it is to hide and get lost in that expanse.

Although the director's job is to create a visualization of these images, it's the writer's job to create a cinematic script that can be translated into these visuals.

THE PROBLEMS OF "MAKING IT COMMERCIAL"

In *Adventures in the Screen Trade*, William Goldman makes the statement, "Nobody knows anything." And that's exactly how many executives and producers feel in this business when they try to figure out what is commercial. It all feels subjective. Sometimes all they can say is, "I know it when I see it."

It is true that "commercial" is easier to understand after a film is a hit, rather than before. Certainly I do not mean to suggest that what makes something commercial is just a matter of research, analysis, and psyching out the audience. Studio research departments have proven that this is not the case, since often their research "proved" that no one would go see *Star Wars*, or that *E.T.* had little appeal, or that *Crocodile Dundee* had no hopes of doing well with American audiences.

Unfortunately, since no one is sure what makes something commercial, there is often an unwillingness to think about the commercial elements at all. Sometimes it leads writers to say, "I just want to express myself," thereby giving no consideration to whether they're communicating with audiences. Sometimes it leads to executives turning the responsibility of making a script commercial over to the director, writer, and actors, hoping that somehow they'll know enough about what they're doing to pull off a commercial project. And with everyone involved in the project, it can lead to bypassing one's own feelings and intuitions that can give clues about how audiences will respond.

Ultimately, "commercial" has much to do with one's own connection to the project. If you feel passionately about a story, if there's some profound connection you are personally making with the subject matter and characters and the journey, then you have made a start at finding what's "commercial." In the final analysis, the executives who say, "It's all subjective" are probably correct. It all begins with our personal connections to the story and with communicating the feelings and excitement that makes us want to share that special story.

131

APPLICATION

Finding the connections with the audience is often difficult. These commercial aspects are not always clear. Often the theme is unclear or underdeveloped. Sometimes there are several themes that conflict with each other, and the job of rewriting is to choose what it is you really want to say.

One way to explore these elements is through a technique called *clustering*. Think of the main idea of your script: "Boy goes back to the past in a time machine," or "Alien lands on Earth," or "Men go after man-eating shark." Place this idea in the middle of a circle and then begin thinking of all the associations you have with this idea. Think through the personal aspects (descriptive and prescriptive). Does it relate to social trends? What's universal about it? Does it remind you of other stories?

Building a cluster around the idea behind *Jaws* might look something like the following chart.

As you begin to cluster around your one-line idea, others will emerge. Some will seem more interesting to you than others. You'll begin to see the relationship of one idea to another. And you'll become clearer about what you really want to say in your script.

As you continue to cluster, certain ways of executing the idea will come to mind. For instance, if you wanted to stress the belonging needs and the theme of community, you would look for ways to build up relationships between characters. Perhaps you originally intended to only have two men in the boat going after the shark. As you explored your idea, you decided to add a third and to build up their relationship by adding other scenes on the boat.

As you become clearer about your theme, ask yourself:

Can I say my theme in one line? Does my story serve my theme, and does my theme serve my story?

Is my theme expressed through character and through action, rather than just through dialogue? Do my

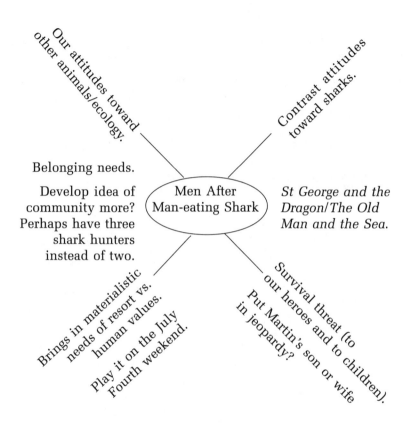

Our attitudes toward other animals/ecology.

Belonging needs.

Develop idea of community more? Perhaps have three shark hunters instead of two.

Men After Man-eating Shark

Contrast attitudes toward sharks.

St George and the Dragon/The Old Man and the Sea.

Brings in materialistic needs of resort vs. human values. Play it on the July Fourth weekend.

Survival threat (to our heroes and to children). Put Martin's son or wife in jeopardy?

images help expand my theme? Have I stayed away from having a character "give a message" to the audience?

Have I been willing to give up a smaller theme if it conflicts with the main theme of the story?

Have I thought through my own personal connections to the theme? Have I considered ways that the audience might respond, given their demographics?

Once you begin to find these connections between audience and material, between your story and your theme, there is one more connection you need to explore. This is the deepest connection possible in a story—creating the myth.

Chapter Eight

Creating the Myth

A ll of us have similar experiences. We share in the life jour-ney of growth, development, and transformation. We live the same stories, whether they involve the search for a perfect mate, coming home, the search for fulfillment, going after an ideal, achieving the dream, or hunting for a precious treasure. Whatever our culture, there are universal stories that form the basis for all our particular stories. The trappings might be different, the twists and turns that create suspense might change from culture to culture, the particular characters may take different forms, but underneath it all, it's the same story, drawn from the same experiences.

Many of the most successful films are based on these universal stories. They deal with the basic journey we take in life. We identify with the heroes because we were once heroic (descriptive) or because we wish we could do what the hero does (prescriptive). When James Bond saves the world, or Shane saves the family from the evil ranchers, or the Amish save John from Schaeffer, we identify with the character and subconsciously recognize the story as having some connection with our own lives. It's the same story as the fairy tales about getting the three golden hairs from the devil or finding the treasure and winning the princess. And it's not all that different a story from the caveman killing the woolly beast or the Roman slave gaining his freedom through skill and courage. These are our stories—personally and collectively—and the most successful films contain these universal experiences.

Some of these stories are "search" stories. They address our desire to find some kind of rare and wonderful treasure. This might include the search for outer values such as job, relationship, or success; or for inner values such as respect, security, self-expression, love, or home. But it's all a similar search.

Some of these stories are "hero" stories. They come from our own experiences of overcoming adversity, as well as our desire to do great and special acts. We root for the hero and celebrate when he or she achieves the goal because we know that the hero's journey is in many ways similar to our own.

We call these stories **myths**. Myths are the common stories at the root of our universal existence. They're found in all cultures and in all literature, ranging from the Greek myths to fairy tales, legends, and stories drawn from all of the world's religions.

A myth is a story that is "more than true." Many stories are true because one person, somewhere, at some time, lived it. It is based on fact. But a myth is more than true because it is lived by all of us, at some level. It's a story that connects and speaks to us all.

Some myths are true stories that attain mythic significance because the people involved seem larger than life, and seem to live their lives more intensely than common folk. Martin Luther King, Jr., Gandhi, Sir Edmund Hillary, and Lord Mountbatten personify the types of journeys we identify with because we've taken similar journeys—even if only in a very small way.

Other myths revolve around make-believe characters who might capsulate for us the sum total of many of our journeys. Some of these make-believe characters might seem similar to the characters we meet in our dreams. Or they might be a composite of types of characters we've met.

In both cases, the myth is the "story beneath the story." It's the universal pattern that shows us that Gandhi's journey toward independence and Sir Edmund Hillary's journey to the top of Mount Everest contain many of the same dramatic beats. And these beats are the same beats that Rambo takes to set free the MIAs, that Indiana Jones takes to find the Lost Ark, and that Luke Skywalker takes to defeat the Evil Empire.

In *Hero with a Thousand Faces,* Joseph Campbell traces the elements that form the hero myth. This criteria has been applied to the film *Star Wars* by seminar leaders Chris Vogler and Thomas Schlesinger, as well as in conversations between Joseph Campbell and Bill Moyers in the PBS series, "The Power of Myth." The myth within the story helps explain why millions went to see this film again and again."

The hero myth has specific story beats that occur in all hero stories. They show who the hero is, what the hero needs, and how the story and character interact in order to create a transformation. The journey toward heroism is a process. This universal process forms the spine of all the particular stories, such as the *Star Wars* trilogy.

THE HERO MYTH

1. In most hero stories, the hero is introduced in ordinary surroundings, in a mundane world, doing mundane things. Generally, the hero begins as a nonhero: innocent, young, simple, or humble. In *Star Wars,* the first time we see Luke Skywalker, he's unhappy about having to do his chores, which consists of picking out some new droids for work. He wants to go out and have fun. He wants to leave his planet and go to the Academy, but he's stuck. This is the set-up of most myths. This is how we meet the hero before the call to adventure.

2. Then something new enters the hero's life. It's a catalyst that sets the story into motion. It might be the German attack in *The African Queen* or the holograph of Princess Leia in *Star Wars*. Whatever form it takes, it's a new ingredient that pushes the hero into an extraordinary adventure. With this call, the stakes are established, and a problem is introduced that demands a solution.

3. Many times, however, the hero doesn't want to leave. The hero is reluctant, afraid of the unknown, uncertain, perhaps, if s/he is up to the challenge. In *Star Wars*, Luke receives a double call to adventure: First, from Princess Leia in the holograph, and then through Obi-Wan Kenobi, who says he needs Luke's help. But Luke is not ready to go. He returns home, only to find that the Imperial Stormtroopers have burned his farmhouse and slaughtered his family. Now he is personally motivated, ready to enter into the adventure.

4. In any journey, the hero usually receives help, and the help often comes from unusual sources. In many fairy tales, an old woman, a dwarf, a witch, or a wizard helps the hero. The hero achieves the goal because of this help and because the hero is receptive to what this person has to give.

There are a number of fairy tales in which the first and second son are sent to complete a task, but they ignore the helpers, often scorning them. Many times they are severely punished for their lack of humility and unwillingness to accept help. Then the third son, the hero, comes along. He receives the help, accomplishes the task, and often wins the princess.

In *Star Wars*, Obi-Wan Kenobi is a perfect example of the "helper" character. He's a kind of mentor to Luke, one who teaches him the Way of the Force and whose teachings continue even after his death. This mentor character appears in most hero stories. He's the person who has special knowledge, special information, and special skills. This might be the prospector in *The Treasure of the Sierra Madre,* or the psychiatrist in *Ordinary People,* or Quint in *Jaws,* who knows all about sharks, or the Good Witch of the North, who gives Dorothy the ruby slippers in *The Wizard of Oz. In Star Wars*, Obi-Wan gives Luke the light saber that was the special weapon of the Jedi Knight. With this, Luke is ready to move forward and do his training and meet adventure.

5. The hero is now ready to move into the special world, ready to change from the ordinary into the extraordinary. This starts the hero's transformation and sets up the obstacles that must be surmounted to reach the goal. Usually, this happens at the first turning point of the story and leads into Act Two development. In *Stars Wars*, Obi-Wan and Luke search for a pilot to take them to the planet of Alderan, so that Obi-Wan can deliver the plans to Princess Leia's father. These plans are essential to the survival of the Rebel Forces. With this action, the adventure is ready to begin.

6. Now begin all the tests and obstacles necessary to overcome the enemy and accomplish the hero's goals. In fairy tales, this often means getting past witches, outwitting the devil, avoiding robbers, or confronting evil. In Homer's *Odyssey*, it means blinding the Cyclops, escaping from the island of the Lotus-Eaters, resisting the temptation of the singing Sirens, and surviving a shipwreck. In *Star Wars,* innumerable adventures confront Luke. He and his cohorts must run to the Millenium Falcon, narrowly escaping the Stormtroopers before jumping into hyperspace. They must evade capture on the Death Star, rescue the Princess, and even survive a garbage crusher.

7. At some point in the story, the hero often hits rock bottom. He often has a "death experience," leading to a type of rebirth. In *Star Wars*, Luke seems to have died when the serpent in the garbage-masher pulls him under, but he's saved just in time to ask R2D2 to stop the masher before they're crushed. This is often the "black moment" at the second turning point, the point when the worst is confronted, and the action now moves toward the exciting conclusion.

8. Now, the hero seizes the sword and takes possession of the treasure. He is now in charge, but he still has not completed the journey. Here, Luke has the Princess and the plans, but the final confrontation is yet to begin. This starts the third-act escape scene, leading to the final climax.

9. The road back is often the chase scene. In many fairy tales, this is the point where the devil chases the hero and the hero has the last obstacles to overcome before really being free and safe. His challenge is to take what he has learned and integrate it into his daily life. He must return to renew the mundane world. In *Star Wars*, Darth Vader is in hot pursuit, planning to blow up the Rebel Planet.

10. Since every hero story is essentially a transformation story, we need to see the hero changed at the end, resurrected into a new type of life. He must face the final ordeal before being "reborn" as the hero, proving his courage and becoming transformed. This is the point, in many fairy tales, where the Miller's Son becomes the King and marries the Princess. In *Star Wars*, Luke has survived, becoming quite a different person from the innocent young man he was in Act One.

At this point, the hero returns and is reintegrated into his society. In *Star Wars*, Luke has destroyed the Death Star, and he receives his great reward.

This is a classic "Hero Story." We might call this example a *mission* or *task myth*, where the person has to complete a task, but the task itself is not the real treasure. The real reward for Luke is the love of the Princess and the safe, new world he had helped create.

A myth can have many variations. We see variations on this myth in James Bond films (although they lack much of the depth because the hero is not transformed), and in *Jaws* where the shark must be destroyed, or in *Places of the Heart*, where Edna overcomes obstacles to achieve family stability.

The *treasure myth* is another variation on this theme, whether the hero's journey is for a treasure or to complete a task, the elements remain the same. The humble, reluctant hero is called to an adventure. The hero is helped by a variety of unique characters. S/he must overcome a series of obstacles that transform him or her in the process, and then faces the final challenge that draws on inner and outer resources.

THE HEALING MYTH

Although the hero myth is the most popular story, many myths involve healing. In these stories, some character is "broken" and must leave home to become whole again.

The universal experience behind these healing stories is our psychological need for rejuvenation, for balance. The journey of the hero into exile is not all that different from the weekend in Palm Springs, or the trip to Hawaii to get away from it all, or lying still in a hospital bed for some weeks to heal. In all cases, something is out of balance and the mythic journey moves toward wholeness.

Being broken can take several forms. It can be physical, emotional, or psychological. Usually, it's all three. In the process of being exiled or hiding out in the forest, the desert, or even the Amish farm in *Witness*, the person becomes whole, balanced and receptive to love. Love in these stories is both a healing force and a reward.

Think of John Book in *Witness*. In Act One, we see a frenetic, insensitive man, afraid of commitment, critical, and unreceptive to the feminine influences in his life. John is suffering from an "inner wound" that he doesn't know about. When he receives an "outer wound" from a gun shot, it forces him into exile, which begins his process of transformation.

At the beginning of Act Two, we see John delirious and close to death. This is a movement into the unconscious, a movement from the rational, active police life of Act One into a mysterious, feminine, more intuitive world. Since John's "inner problem" is the lack of balance with his feminine side, this delirium begins the process of transformation.

Later in Act Two, we see John beginning to change. He moves from his highly independent lifestyle toward the collective, communal life of his Amish hosts. John now gets up early to milk the cows and to assist with the chores. He uses his carpentry skills to help with the barn building and to complete the birdhouse. Gradually, he begins to develop relationships with Rachel and her son, Samuel. John's life slows down and he becomes more receptive, learning important lessons about love. In Act Three, John finally sees that the feminine is worth saving and throws down his gun to save Rachel's life. A few beats later, when he has the opportunity to kill Paul, he chooses a nonviolent response instead. Although John doesn't "win" the Princess, he has nevertheless "won" love and wholeness. By the end of the film, we can see that the John Book of Act Three is a different kind of person from the John Book of Act One. He has a different kind of comradeship with his fellow police officers, he's more relaxed, and we can sense that, somehow, this experience has formed a more integrated John Book.

COMBINATION MYTHS

Many stories are combinations of several different myths. Think of *Ghostbusters*, an outrageous comedy about three men saving the city of New York from ghosts. Now think of the story of "Pandora's Box." It's about the woman who let loose all manner of evil upon the earth by opening a box that she was told not to touch. In *Ghostbusters*, the EPA man is a Pandora figure. By shutting off the power to the containment center, he inadvertently unleashes all the ghosts upon New York City. Combine the story of "Pandora's Box" with a hero story, and notice that we have our three heroes battling the Marshmallow Man. One of them also "gets the Princess" when Dr. Peter Venkman finally receives the affections of Dana Barrett. By looking at these combinations, it is apparent that even *Ghostbusters* is more than "just a comedy."

Tootsie is a type of reworking of many Shakespearean stories in which a woman has to dress as a man in order to accomplish a certain task. These Shakespearean stories are reminiscent of many fairy tales, where the hero becomes invisible or takes on another persona or wears a specific disguise to hide his or her real qualities. In the stories of "The Twelve Dancing Princesses" or "The Man In the Bearskin," disguise is necessary to achieve a goal. Combine these elements with the transformation themes of the hero myth where a hero (such as Michael) must overcome many obstacles to his success as an actor and a human being. It's not difficult to understand why the *Tootsie* story hooks us.

ARCHETYPES

A myth includes certain characters that we see in many stories. These characters are called *archetypes*. They can be thought of as the original "pattern" or "character type" that will be found on the hero's journey. Archetypes take many forms, but they tend to fall within specific categories.

Earlier, we discussed some of the helpers who give advice to help the hero—such as the wise old man who possesses special knowledge and often serves as a mentor to the hero.

The female counterpart of the wise old man is the good mother. Whereas the wise old man has superior knowledge, the good mother is known for her nurturing qualities and for her intuition. This figure often gives the hero particular objects to help on the journey. It might be a protective amulet or the ruby slippers that Dorothy receives in *The Wizard of Oz* from the Good Witch of the North. Sometimes in fairy tales it's a cloak to make the person invisible or ordinary objects that become extraordinary, as in "The Girl of Courage," an Afghan fairy tale about a maiden who receives a comb, a whetstone, and a mirror to help defeat the devil.

Many myths contain a *shadow figure*. This is a character who is the opposite of the hero. Sometimes this figure helps the hero on the journey; other times this figure opposes the hero.

The shadow figure can be the negative side of the hero which could be the dark and hostile brother in _Cain and Abel_, the stepsisters in _Cinderella_, or the Robber Girl in _The Snow Queen_. The shadow figure can also help the hero, as the whore with the heart of gold who saves the hero's life or provides balance to his idealization of woman.

Many myths contain _animal archetypes_ that can be positive or negative figures. In _St. George and the Dragon_, the dragon is the negative force, which is a violent and ravaging animal—not unlike the shark in _Jaws_. But in many stories, animals help the hero. Sometimes there are talking donkeys, or a dolphin that saves the hero, or magical horses or dogs.

The _trickster_ is a mischievous archetypical figure who is always causing chaos, disturbing the peace, and generally being an anarchist. The trickster uses wit and cunning to achieve his or her ends. Sometimes the trickster is a harmless prankster or a "bad boy" who is funny and enjoyable. More often, the trickster is a con man, as in _The Sting,_ or the devil, as in _The Exorcist_, who demanded all the skills of the priest to outwit him. The _Till Eulenspiegel_ stories revolve around the trickster, as do the Spanish picaresque novels. Even the _Tale of Tom Sawyer_ has a trickster motif. In all countries, there are stories that revolve around this figure, whose job it is to outwit.

"MYTHIC" PROBLEMS AND SOLUTIONS

We all grew up with myths. Most of us heard or read fairy tales when we were young. Some of us may have read Bible stories or stories from other religions or other cultures. These stories are part of us. And the best way to work with them is to let them come out naturally as you write the script.

Of course, some filmmakers are better at this than others. George Lucas and Steven Spielberg have a strong sense of myth and incorporate it into their films. They both have spoken about their love of the stories from childhood and of their desire to bring these types of stories to audiences. Their stories create some of the same sense of wonder and excitement as myths. Many of the necessary psychological beats are part of their stories, deepening the story beyond the ordinary action-adventure.

Myths bring depth to a hero story. If a filmmaker is only thinking about the action and excitement of a story, audiences might fail to connect with the hero's journey. But if the basic beats of the hero's journey are evident, a film will often inexplicably draw audiences, in spite of critics' responses to the film.

Take *Rambo* for instance. Why was this violent, simple story so popular with audiences? I don't think it was because everyone agreed with its politics. I do think Sylvester Stallone is a master at incorporating the American myth into his filmmaking. That doesn't mean that it's done consciously. Somehow, he is naturally in sync with the myth, and the myth becomes integrated into his stories.

Clint Eastwood also does hero stories and gives us the adventure of the myth and the transformation of the myth. Recently, Eastwood's films have given more attention to the transformation of the hero and have been receiving more serious critical attention as a result.

All of these filmmakers—Lucas, Spielberg, Stallone and Eastwood—dramatize the hero myth in their own particular ways. And all of them prove that myths are marketable.

APPLICATION

It is an important part of the writer's or producer's work to continually find opportunities for deepening the themes within a script. Finding the myth beneath the modern story is part of that process.

To find these myths, it's not a bad idea to reread some of Grimm's fairy tales or fairy tales from around the world to begin to get acquainted with various myths. You'll start to see patterns and elements that connect with our human experience.

Also, read Joseph Campbell and Greek mythology. If you're interested in Jungian psychology, you'll find many rich resources within a number of books on the subject. Since Jungian psychology deals with archetypes, you'll find many new characters to draw on for your own work.

With all of these resources to incorporate, it's important to remember that the myth is not a story to force upon a script. It's more a pattern that you can bring out in your own stories when they seem to be heading in the direction of a myth.

As you work, ask yourself:

Do I have a myth working in my script? If so, what beats am I using of the hero's journey? Which ones seem to be missing?

Am I missing characters? Do I need a mentor type? A wise old man? A wizard? Would one of these characters help dimensionalize the hero's journey?

Could I create new emotional dimensions to the myth by starting my character as reluctant, naive, simple, or decidedly "un-heroic"?

Does my character get transformed in the process of the journey?

Have I used a strong three-act structure to support the myth, using the first turning point to move into the adventure and the second turning point to create a dark moment, or a reversal, or even a "near-death" experience?

Don't be afraid to create variations on the myth, but don't start with the myth itself. Let the myth grow naturally from your story. Developing myths are part of the rewriting process. If you begin with the myth, you'll find that your writing becomes rigid, uncreative, and predictable. Working with the myth in the rewriting process will deepen your script, giving it new life as you find the story within the story.

Part Three

Character Development

Chapter Nine

From Motivation to Goal: Finding the Character Spine

Most stories are relatively simple. Their beginnings, middles, and ends can be told in a few words: "E.T. gets caught on Earth and then goes home"; "Marty goes back thirty years in a time machine and returns back to the future"; "Michael dresses as a woman, gets an acting job, and then unmasks."

Stories become complex through the influence of **character**. It's character that impinges on the story, dimensionalizes the story, and moves the story in new directions. With all the idiosyncrasies and willfulness of character, the story changes. Character makes the story compelling.

Think about the characters of Rose and Allnutt in *The African Queen*. If Rose hadn't held the Germans accountable for her brother's death, and hadn't been so angry and determined, the *Louisa* would never have been torpedoed. But Rose's character changed the action of the story. Allnutt's plan was to take it easy for a few days and then come up with a simple plan that would save their lives. Rose wanted to get back at the Germans and do something for her country. Allnutt would not have agreed if Rose the missionary hadn't thrown out his gin and given him the silent treatment until he had to give in. Rose's character caused the story to move in new directions.

Character influences the story because the character, particularly the main one, has a *goal*. There's something the main character wants. This goal gives direction to the story.

At the beginning of the story, something motivates the character to go after this goal. The character then takes certain actions to achieve it. And at the end of most films, the goal is attained.

Just as a storyline has a spine that is determined by the setup, the turning points, and the climax, there is also a **character spine.** The spine of the character is determined by the relationship of **motivation** and **action** to the **goal.** Characters need all of these elements to clearly define who they are, what they want, why they want it, and what actions they're willing to take to get it.

If any of these elements are missing, the character line becomes confused and unfocused. There's no direction. We're unclear who to root for and why we're rooting for someone at all.

MOTIVATION

All of us have watched films where we don't know why the characters do what they do. We've seen films where the hero goes to considerable lengths to save his country, but we've never seen any evidence that the country means anything to him at all.

We've seen films where characters seem irritated, get angry, or fall in love for no apparent reason. In each of these cases, the motivation is weak and unclear. If we don't know why a character is doing something, it's difficult to get involved in the story. As a result, the story loses momentum and we lose interest.

Motivation pushes the character forward into the story. It's a catalyst at the beginning of the story that forces the character to get involved. Like any catalyst, the motivation can be physical, expressed through dialogue, or situational.

A physical action will always give the most push to the story. The escape of Richard Kimble forces Sam Gerard to begin the chase (*The Fugitive*). In *Unforgiven*, the cutting up of the whore forces Will Munny to try to avenge the act. And the appearance of ghosts forces the *Ghostbusters* into action.

These kinds of events catapult the main character into the story. They force the character to become involved in what's to take place. And they do it in a clear, incisive way.

Sometimes a story uses a combination of physical events and dialogue to build up a *situation*, so we sense what's pushing the character, although no specific moment is the catalyst. *Tootsie* builds up the motivation through showing us the struggles that Michael goes through to get a job. His repeated failures motivate him to try anything—including applying for a job as a woman in a soap opera.

Tootsie begins with a montage of several of these casting calls:

INT. A DARKENED THEATRE

                    VOICE
        Michael . . . Dorsey is it?

PULL BACK to hold on MICHAEL looking out toward a darkened auditorium. He is an actor, forty years old. he holds a script.

                    MICHAEL
        That's right.

                    VOICE
        Top of twenty-three.

                    MICHAEL
         (with feeling)
        "Do you know what it was like waking up in
        Paris in the morning? Seeing that empty pil-
        low where . . . wait a minute, cover your
        breasts! Kevin is downstairs! My God—what
        are you?"

PULL BACK to reveal a BURLY STAGE MANAGER, cigar butt in mouth.

> STAGE MANAGER
> "I'm a *woman*. Not Felicia's mother. Not
> Kevin's wife . . . "

> VOICE
> Thank you. That's fine. We're looking for some-
> one a little older.

INT. ANOTHER BARE STAGE—MICHAEL WITH
ANOTHER STAGE MANAGER.

Michael is dressed in cut-offs, a T-shirt, and sneakers.
He plays with a yo-yo.

> MICHAEL
> Mom! Dad! Uncle Pete! Something's wrong
> with Biscuit! I think he's dead.

> VOICE
> (From the darkness)
> Thank you. Thank you. We're looking for
> someone a little younger.

INT. A THIRD BARE STAGE—MICHAEL ALONE ON
STAGE.

Michael angrily slaps the script against his thigh.

> MICHAEL
> Just a second now, could I start again? I just
> didn't start it right.

> VOICE
> (From the darkness)
> No, no, it was very good. Really it was fine.
> You're just the wrong height.

MICHAEL
Well hold it, I can be taller. I've got lifts at
home, it's really easy to add a few . . .

VOICE
No, no, you don't understand, we need someone shorter.

MICHAEL
I don't have to be this tall! I'm wearing lifts—

With the completion of this montage, we understand what's driving Michael. From now on, there is no reason for us to question
why Michael dresses up like a woman to try to get a job.

Sometimes stories rely too much on a character *explaining* motivation, rather than *showing* motivation. This happens
when there is no action to push the character into the story.
Since we don't see any specific action, characters have to explain a reason for their involvement. This works well in novels but is rarely effective in drama. If we can't clearly see what
motivates the character's entrance into the story, chances are
that no amount of explaining is going to help us understand.

Several methods are often used to tell rather than show
motivation, but these are usually ineffective. One is the **expository speech,** the other is the **flashback.**

In many scripts, writers will emphasize the backstory as
the chief motivator for a character's actions. This means that
characters will have long expository speeches talking about the
past as the cause for their present actions. They'll discuss their
background and psychology, giving us information about where
they grew up with long histories of their early life and their parents. Or they might talk about the influences of other characters on their lives at an early age, discussing a favorite aunt or
a villainous uncle. Or they might talk about the trouble they had
two—or fifteen—years ago, meticulously explaining how that
caused them to do something in the present.

Usually these kinds of speeches bog down the script. Sometimes what they talk about isn't relevant to the issue at hand. Other times they fail to show a present motivation that's more important than past information. Many times a writer sees these speeches as revealing character, but character is best revealed through action that advances the story. Scenes that only reveal character fail to give the necessary motivational push to the character. And since drama is image-oriented rather than talk-oriented, anything that tells rather than shows diminishes the dramatic power of the scene.

Flashbacks, in many instances, also are informational rather than dramatic. Generally, flashbacks are used to explain, to give information about the backstory, or to give character information. Many times a writer will explain the use of flashbacks by saying, "I wanted to give you further information about my character. The past seemed relevant to explain the present."

Flashbacks as a means to explain motivation rarely work well. This is true for a number of reasons. First of all, motivation is meant to push the character forward. Flashbacks, by their nature, stop the action because they find the motivation in a distant past, rather than in the immediate present. If the motivation really happened long ago, the character would have been in the story long ago. Real motivation happens in the present time. It might be the last in a series of incidents that happen, but motivation happens when the character is ready. It happens now. It's imminent. It's present.

Flashbacks put the emphasis on details rather than on the dramatic moment. They stress the inner psychology of a character rather than the present actions that force response. They reveal character, but rarely do they motivate character.

This is not to say, "Never use flashbacks." Some flashbacks are necessary for thematic purposes or to serve the style of the film. *Kiss of the Spider Woman* seemed to demand flashbacks to break out of the confinement of the cell. The story of *Stand by Me* is played as a flashback, exploring themes of identity and friendship as an adult looks back on a key incident in his life.

The flashbacks in *The Fugitive* helped unravel the mystery as well as give the audience important facts about the murder. But most good films will emphasize the unfolding of the present as a usable way to reveal motivation.

You might ask, "If I don't use flashbacks or expository speeches to explain the story, then where do I start the story? How do I find that beginning image that sets everything in motion?" Many times you can clarify and focus motivation by placing the main character at a *crisis point* in the beginning of the story. At a crisis point, characters are particularly vulnerable to being thrust in new directions. They are ready for something new to unfold because, in some way, their old world (or old story) has been destroyed and a new story is emerging. Think of Edna in *Places in the Heart* or Rachel in *Witness*. We see them right after the death of their husbands, vulnerable, in need, on the brink of something new ready to happen.

In many of the best films, you will see characters on the brink. In *Ghostbusters*, the three parapsychologists have been fired from their jobs. The crisis point, together with the appearance of the ghosts, catapults them into their new career.

In *Star Wars*, the Death Star is ready to destroy everything valuable. That calls for immediate action from all the good guys.

Gone With the Wind shows a country on the brink of war. This situation motivates the actions that follow.

To work well, motivation needs to be clear. It needs to be focused. It should be expressed through action, not talk. And it's designed to catapult the main character into the story because s/he is at a crisis point in life. Motivation pushes the character. The goal gives direction to that push.

THE GOAL

As a result of the motivation, the character begins to look toward a goal. The main character is heading somewhere. There is something that s/he wants. Just as motivation pushes the character forward in a specific direction, the goal pulls the character toward the climax.

The goal is an essential part of drama. It's not unusual to hear an executive say, "But what does the character want?" Without a clear goal in mind, the story will wander and become hopelessly confused. Without a clear goal, it will be impossible to find the spine of the story.

The goal ties the character in with the climax of the story. The climax is reached by the character going after the goal and achieving it.

But not just any goal will do. In order for a goal to function well, it needs to meet three main requirements.

First of all, something must be at stake in the story that convinces the audience that a great deal will be lost if the main character does not gain the goal. If we don't believe in the necessity of the character gaining the goal, we won't be able to root for that character. Of course, stakes can be anything from survival stakes (*Star Wars*) to belonging stakes (*Places in the Heart*) to self-esteem stakes (*Tootsie*) or even the survival of someone else (*Cocoon*). But we need to clearly understand the goal and understand that it's essential for the character's well-being that it's achieved.

Secondly, a workable goal brings the protagonist in direct conflict with the goals of the antagonist. This conflict sets the context for the entire story and strengthens the main character because s/he now has a worthy opponent. Obviously attaining the goal will not be easy because someone else is intent on making sure that the protagonist doesn't achieve it.

Thirdly, the goal should be sufficiently difficult to achieve so that the character changes while moving toward it. The strongest characters will achieve some extra dimension by this journey. In some way they'll be transformed, because the goal cannot be achieved without some kind of character change. The movement toward the goal will have its effect on the characters involved. It will make demands of them. And the only way they can gain what they want will be to allow those changes to happen. The character must discover courage or resourcefulness or determination. Without achieving some kind of character change, the goal would not be possible.

ACTION

The method by which the character achieves the goal demonstrates the strength and sincerity of the character. People who say that they want something, but won't do anything to get it, are not sincere. These characters are difficult to believe in. They lack credibility. So the character has to take specific actions in pursuit of the goal. The stronger the actions and the stronger the barriers to achieve the goal, the stronger the character.

Naturally, obstacles and actions come in many different forms. Actions can range from investigating and trying to find out (*North by Northwest*) to shooting (*Dirty Harry*) to capturing and destroying (*Ghostbusters*) to the tearing down and the building up of a land (*Gone With the Wind*). In each of these, the action is clear, dramatic, and each beat moves closer to a final goal.

If we were to look at motivations, actions, and goals in relation to films, it might look like this:

Motivation	Action	Goal
Witness The murder of a police officer forces John Book to	keep Rachel & Samuel in Philadelphia, to show Samuel a line-up, mug shots, to talk to Paul, to hide out at an Amish Farm, to phone his partner, to threaten Paul in order to	expose the villains.

Back to the Future
A beefed-up De Lorean forces Marty into the past.

He overcomes Mother's advances, seeks out the Professor, fights with Biff, dresses as Darth Vader to motivate George to ask Lorraine out. He cajoles, persuades, manipulates, in order to survive and get back to the future.

The African Queen
Germans destroying the village and killing her brother motivates Rose to go through rapids, through shootings, through weeds. She swims underwater to help repair the boat and forces Allnutt to become her partner in order to destroy the *Louisa.*

In these films, the motivation is clear, the action is strong, and the goal is sufficiently compelling to pull the character forward toward the accomplishment of the objective.

PROBLEMS THAT OCCUR WITH THE CHARACTER SPINE

Unclear motivation, or lack of it, is one of the most common problems in films. We've all seen many films where we keep asking "Why?" "Why is the character doing that? Why don't they do this instead?"

After a screening of *The Mosquito Coast*, several audience members asked, "But why would the wife stay with Allie without protesting his actions?" After *The Mission,* some people asked, "Why was the mission so important to the natives? Why were they willing to die for it?"

Sometimes the answers to motivation are within the film, but as audience members we don't hear them. The film goes quickly, we don't hear all the dialogue, or we don't understand the relationship of one piece of motivating information with another.

Sometimes a motivation needs to be repeated more than once for audiences to catch it. Many times motivations are clear only when they're expressed through action, image *and* dialogue.

Motivational information can be difficult to incorporate into a film. Setting up a story and introducing a character, while also creating a dramatic opening image, demands careful integration of many elements. Many times, character motivation gets shortchanged in the process. It's difficult to know how much backstory and how much exposition is necessary for an audience to get with the story. Beginning writers tend to include too much. Veteran screenwriters sometimes err on the other side, leaving out an image or a piece of dialogue that might have made all the difference.

Problems with the character spine will more often be found with motivation and actions than with the goal. Usually the goal is clear. However, sometimes a character does not take sufficient action to achieve the goal.

We go to the films to see a good story and to see characters doing, not just talking. Yet some characters are passive characters. This can be workable for part of the film, but if a main character remains passive for most of the film, we lose interest. If they don't care enough to exert effort to achieve the goal, we don't care. Somewhere by the midpoint of the script (if not before), the character has to begin acting upon the story rather than being victimized by it.

In some films, the passivity of the main character gives a feeling that the character's story is separate from the main story of the film. This was true to some extent in *The Morning After* with Jane Fonda. The story material related to the murder— "Who did it? Why did they do it? Will they get caught? Will they succeed in framing Alexandra?" But the film was essentially a character film. And Alexandra's actions did not cause the climax to happen.

This created a few problems that were expressed in various ways in several reviews. The story behind the scenes about the murderers had the most movement to it, but we caught very few glimpses of it since the information about the murderers was played as a small subplot. Since the emphasis was on character and character transformation, the main character had very little action to do for most of the film, even though the problem demanded action that would lead to a solution. The main character was a victim of the storyline, rather than an active participant forcing the killer's hand, or discovering key information, or influencing an effective confession. Since the main character didn't cause the climax to happen, the relationship between story spine and character spine was weakened.

The intention of *The Morning After* seemed to be to create a different kind of film. The writer (James Hicks) stayed away from the usual detective/mystery/murder story where a woman gets pulled into an investigation by the macho cop, thereby solving the mystery. And some of these choices did pay off, evidenced by many rave reviews about the acting and the strong transformational arc of Fonda's character.

But this film, like others, demonstrates the many balancing acts a writer needs to do. A strong film needs a clear story line without becoming predictable. It needs an integration of the plots and subplots. And it needs that clear and concise character spine of motivation, action, and goal.

APPLICATION

The first job of a character rewrite is to make sure that you've created a strong character through-line. In many scripts, simply too much information is covering up the clear motivation, action, and goal of a character. Uncovering and clarifying this character spine is a process of tearing down some beats and building up others.

If you feel that your script is bogged down by too much talk and not enough action, you might want to begin the rewrite by removing all the expository sections. Look for any places where characters are explaining themselves. Look for any section of dialogue where characters have long speeches that give psychological sketches about the backstory. Take those sections out of the script.

Then check for flashbacks. If any of them are expository, rather than dramatic, remove them also.

Now look at the beats that are left in the story. Is there a clear catalyst that motivates the character into the story? If not, see if there's a crisis point you can create to force a character into action. Find a visual way to show that crisis point.

Look at the actions that are part of your story. Perhaps, with the removal of some of the exposition, there are few left. If so, look back to the expository passages you removed to see if any actions are discussed or implied that could be played out by your character. If so, substitute those actions for the expository dialogue you've removed.

Look at the goal of your character. Is the goal set up in Act One? Is it clear? When the character reaches the goal, do we know that the story is finished? Are the climax and the goal the same (which is almost always true)? Are there clear goals on both your plot and subplot lines? Are all of them resolved toward the end of the script?

Once you have focused on the images and actions of your story, look back to the sections you removed. Within the expository passages, perhaps even with the flashbacks, there might be pertinent information that needs to be in the script. If these sections are long speeches, see if you can reduce the pertinent information to a sentence or two. Rather than placing it all in one scene, thereby creating a talky scene that will slow down the story, use these small expository sections sparingly throughout the script, particularly in Acts One and Two. If some of them reveal character through talk, try to find an image or an action that you can substitute for the dialogue.

By uncovering the spine of the story and character through removing information, it will be easier to see what's slowing down the story and what's essential to give clarity and movement.

Then ask yourself the following questions of your script:

Is my character motivated by action or by talk? Is there a clear moment when my character enters into the story? Do we know why s/he's begins to act?

What is my character's goal? Is it sufficiently compelling to move my character through three acts?

Is my character active or passive in achieving the goal? Does the action meet the needs of the storyline? If it's an action-adventure, do I use strong, dramatic actions? If it's relational, do I find more subtle ways to move the action?

If I've used flashbacks, long expository speeches, or backstory, is it absolutely essential? Whenever possible, do I condense or cut this material?

Can I clearly discuss my character spine in a few words? Is it clear how the character spine intersects with the spine of the story?

Many scripts, particularly by beginning writers, are bogged down with excess information. Once this information is removed, often a script picks up energy immediately, and what may have seemed like a dead script might start exhibiting signs of life and vitality.

Motivation, action, and goal will give drive and direction to a script. But there's another element that needs to be added. That's the lifeblood of drama—conflict.

Chapter Ten

Finding the Conflict

It's not unusual for an executive to tell a writer, "Make it strong!" or "It needs more punch!" or "It's flat!" Usually what the executive is really saying is, "It lacks conflict!"

Conflict is the basis of drama. It's the stuff by which drama is made. A novel can be interior and "soft," a poem can be flowery and appreciative, but drama needs grit, punch, and "fight." That's true whether you're doing an action-adventure, a comedy-romance, a warm sitcom, or a sci-fi fantasy. Conflict is the key ingredient of any dramatic form. Drama doesn't focus on characters playing nice with each other. In drama, characters don't shy away from confrontation. In good drama, characters enter into a dynamic relationship that emphasizes differences. They confront, fight, scrap, argue, persuade, and try to force their point of view, their decisions, their actions on people who don't see things in the same way.

Conflict happens when two characters have mutually exclusive goals at the same time. One character will win, and one will lose. During the course of the story, we watch the protagonist and antagonist battle to achieve their goals. Other characters also come into conflict with them, creating relational conflicts within individual scenes.

Conflict can come in many sizes and shapes. There are different types of conflicts, and some conflicts are better material for drama than others. Fights, arguments, and car chases are not the only ways to express conflict. Good scripts have a wide range of conflict expression and play more than one type of conflict throughout the story.

There are five types of conflict situations to be found in stories: *inner, relational, social, situational,* and *cosmic.* Some of these are more workable than others. And some are better suited to the dramatic form.

INNER CONFLICT

When characters are unsure of themselves, or their action, or even what they want, they are suffering from inner conflict. Inner conflict works well in novels, when a character can confide in the reader, sharing insecurities and uncertainties. It tends, however, to be more problematical in dramas.

Sometimes screenplays use a voice-over or an expository statement to express inner conflict. Unless these are used carefully, they can easily make a story talky.

Sometimes a character expresses inner conflict by confiding feelings to someone else. If used sparingly, this can be workable. However, to work well, this inner conflict needs to be projected outward onto someone else. In *Tootsie*, Michael has a short speech confiding his feelings about his new persona—Dorothy—to his roommate Jeff:

> MICHAEL
> I just wish I *looked* prettier. I feel that she's
> (Dorothy) such a beautiful person. Maybe if I
> give her a softer hair style . . .

Notice how brief this confidence is. Michael could have continued *telling* his feelings and insecurities to Jeff. Instead the inner conflict immediately opens up and becomes more relational, as Michael and Jeff confront the new situation of Dorothy.

The phone rings. Jeff leans for it.

                    MICHAEL
          Don't answer that!

                    JEFF
          Why?

                    MICHAEL
          It could be for Dorothy.

                    JEFF
          You gave them this number?

                    MICHAEL
          I had to! The show may have to get hold of me
          if they change the schedule.

                    JEFF
          I'll answer it and see.

                    MICHAEL
          No! I don't want them to think Dorothy lives
          with a guy. It's wrong for my character!

                    JEFF
          What if it's for me? It could be important! You
          answer it as Dorothy.

                    MICHAEL
          I can't answer it as Dorothy! What if it's Sandy?

>   JEFF
> What if it's Diane? How do I explain a woman
> here?

The phone stops ringing. Michael heads back to the table.

>   MICHAEL
> All right, I'm sorry. We'll get a service.

>   JEFF
>   (rises, picks up coat)
> That takes three days. Look, I didn't complain
> when you put a foil through the couch just un-
> der my arm, when you were Cyrano. Or when
> you stuffed underwear into your shirt for a
> hump, and went running around ranting about
> this being a bell tower! But I don't understand
> why I should sit here pretending I'm not home
> because you're not "that kind of girl"!

And with that Jeff leaves the apartment.

Here we see a key to using inner conflict—*project it out-ward onto a person or an object*. By projecting it outward some-where else, the conflict becomes relational. As a result, we can more easily watch the drama unfold.

For instance, if I were frustrated about my job, I might come home and kick the dog. As a result, the dog bites me. Now the conflict has been projected outward, and the conflict is between the dog and me.

RELATIONAL CONFLICT

Most conflict centers on the mutually exclusive goals of the pro-tagonist and the antagonist. In *Witness*, the conflict is essentially between John Book and Paul Schaeffer. In *Ghostbusters*, Dr. Peter

Venkman and the EPA man are in conflict over how to handle the ghosts in the containment center. In *Unforgiven*, the key conflict is between Will Munny and the sheriff. In *The Silence of the Lambs*, the key conflict is between Clarice Starling (representing the FBI's desire to find the serial killer) and the serial killer, who wants to remain unexposed.

The major conflict in *The African Queen* is between Rose and Allnutt, and their different opinions about what to do after the death of her brother. This conflict gets the story rolling. Rose begins the conflict by suggesting that they make a torpedo and get back at the Germans for killing her brother and destroying the village.

> ALLNUTT
> But what are we talkin' about, anyway.
> There ain't nothin' to torpedo.
> 'Cause *The African Queen's* the only boat
> on the river.

> ROSE
> Oh yes there is.

> ALLNUTT
> Is what?

> ROSE
> Is something to torpedo.

> ALLNUTT
> An' what's that, Miss?

> ROSE
> *The Louisa.*

> ALLNUTT
> Don't talk silly, Miss. You can't do
> that. Honest you can't. I told you
> before, we can't get down the river.

>   ROSE
>   Spengler did.
>
>   ALLNUTT
>   In a canoe, Miss!
>
>   ROSE
>   If a German did it, we can too.

And, of course, Rose wins this conflict—and they're off to torpedo *The Louisa*.

Of course, throughout the story, there are other conflicts— over Allnutt's drinking, over who will sleep in the rain, over how to get past the rapids, over how to get out of the marsh. And, as the story progresses, the conflict and threat with the Germans intensifies as Rose and Allnutt resolve their conflicts and fall in love.

SOCIETAL CONFLICT

Many Movies-of-the-week and feature films deal with conflict between a person and a group. The group might be a bureaucracy, a government, a gang, a family, an agency, a corporation, an army, or even a country. Think of the many films that pit a person against a larger system: *The Killing Fields,* about Dith Pran against the Khmer Rouge; *Star Wars*, where Luke, Princess Leia, and Han Solo stand against the Evil Empire; *Out of Africa*, where part of the conflict is with British-run colonies. Whenever the themes have to do with justice, or corruption, or oppression, chances are that the conflict is societal.

In most social conflicts, one or two people usually represent a larger group. In *The African Queen*, Rose could not take on the entire German nation, but she could try to battle the representation of Germany—the ship, *The Louisa*. In *Gone With the*

Wind, the Civil War and those "damn Yankees" get in the way of Scarlett attaining her goals because the war, at any time, might kill Scarlett's beloved Ashley Wilkes. But specific people at various times personalize the conflict. Rhett Butler won't give Scarlett money to save Tara, the Atlanta Charity Bazaar won't let her dance, and a Yankee soldier tries to steal her valuables. Each of these situations dimensionalizes and focuses the larger conflict. If the conflict occurs between the person and the group, it's in danger of becoming too abstract. As a result, the story might begin with social conflict, but soon it becomes specific, again pitting one person against another.

In *Jaws*, the conflict is actually between Martin Brody and the town leaders, but the conflict quickly moves from Martin-against-the-group to the more specific conflict of Martin-against-Vaughn. This conflict forms the focus of the first half of the film, before the exciting man-against-beast conflict in the last half of the film.

This scene begins shortly after the attack from the first shark, which kills a swimmer. Larry Vaughn, the Mayor, plus several citizens, enter.

> VAUGHN
> What have you got there, Lenny?

> HENDRICKS
> We had a shark attack at South Chop this morning, Mayor. Fatal. Gotta batten down the beach.

Hendricks continues to make a sign about closing down the beach. Vaughn, Ben Meadows, and the coroner Santos, plus two selectmen, exchange horrified looks, but we get the impression that it is not in response to the shark-attack news.

> VAUGHN
> Martin, are you going to shut down the beach
> on your own authority?

                    BRODY
Do I need any more authority?

                    MEADOWS
Technically, you need the instruction of a civic
ordinance, or a special meeting of the town
selectmen . . .

                    VAUGHN
That's just going by the book. We're just a little
anxious that you're rushing into something serious here. This is your first summer.

                    BRODY
Now tell me something I don't know.

                    VAUGHN
All I'm saying is that Amity is a summer town.
We need summer dollars, and if they can't
swim here, they'll use the beaches at Cape Cod
or Long Island.

                    BRODY
So we should set out a smorgasbord?

                    MEADOWS
We're not even sure what it was.

                    BRODY
What else could've done that?

                    VAUGHN
  (to Doctor Santos)
Boat propellor?

                    DOCTOR
I think, possibly . . . sure. A boating accident.

VAUGHN

Some weekend tramp accidently goes swimming too far, she's a little drunk, a fishing boat
comes along . . .

BRODY

Doctor, you're the one who told me what it
was!

DOCTOR

I was wrong. We'll have to amend the report.

VAUGHN

It's all psychological anyway. You yell "barra-
cuda" and everyone says "huh?" You yell
"shark" and we've got a panic on our hands.
I think we all agree we don't need a panic this
close to the Fourth of July.

By this point, the conflict has been clearly laid out—
Brody's integrity and concern for safety versus the town leaders' concern for a commercially successful summer.

SITUATIONAL CONFLICT

In the 1970s, there were many disaster films where characters
had to confront life-and-death situations. Although the situations created tension and suspense, much of the conflict was
still carried relationally. In the *Airport* films, or *The Poseidon
Adventure,* or *The Towering Inferno,* or *Earthquake,* or even *A
Night to Remember,* the situation becomes a pressure cooker,
relational conflicts developing as characters disagree about how
to best survive. Within each scene, different points of view
emerge. Some characters panic, others become leaders, trying
to persuade the group to follow them. Usually, conflicts are fur-

ther individualized, as family members struggle with whether to leave a dying husband or wife, children decide to disobey parents, or age-old conflicts within the family emerge under the pressure.

Without these relational conflicts, situational conflict would be difficult to sustain for any length of time. We can only fight so long against a hurricane, blizzard, fire, or sinking ship. Like other forms of conflict, situational conflict needs to be personal and relational in order to keep us involved.

COSMIC CONFLICT

On very rare occasions, conflict is carried between a character and God—or the devil—or an invisible human being. I'm not talking here about God or Satan being humanized, as in *The Devil and Daniel Webster*. In a play such as this, the conflict is relational rather than cosmic because it's essentially a conflict between two human beings.

Cosmic conflict occurs between a character and a supernatural force. King Lear rages against these powers. Salieri in *Amadeus* declares war on God for creating the brilliant Mozart. *Job* (both the Biblical story and the play) questions and argues with the cosmic force.

But in each of these occasions, conflict is projected onto a human being. Salieri might be angry at God, but he takes it out on Mozart. King Lear might rage against cosmic injustice, but the immediate cause of his problems are his two daughters, who plot against him. And Job has as many arguments with his friends as he has with God.

In order to watch the conflict unfold, we need to see the character project his problems with an invisible force onto a human being who just happens to be in the way.

PROBLEMS WITH CONFLICT

Problems with conflict fall into many categories. Sometimes there are too many conflicts, so it's unclear what the main issue is. Sometimes there are too many antagonists, so the main character is battling too many opponents and doesn't have a clear focus. Sometimes conflict changes from one section of the script to the next. And sometimes the story lacks conflict. It might have interesting and watchable scenes, but there's no compelling through-line to give cohesiveness to the story.

Problems in conflict are particularly prevalent when translating a novel into a script. Most novels are narratives. The novel takes us into the psychology of the character. We learn how they think and feel, what they value. We see how they grapple with issues. And we get insight into their insecurities and obsessions and concerns. This makes for interesting reading and interesting characters, but it also causes problems in the translation to film.

In most novels, the conflict is inner rather than relational. Sometimes there are too many conflicts because of the epic nature of the book. Sometimes the major conflict is not workable for a film because it's too abstract or too intellectual or not of sufficient interest to mass audiences.

Often a film becomes more of a narrative than a drama with a clear conflict from beginning to end. You can see this narrative quality in a number of ways.

Many films use voice-overs, which is a literary device. The voice-over reflections by Charlie in *The Mosquito Coast*, the narrator who remembers the past in *Stand by Me* (from the story *The Body* by Stephen King), or the voice-over that began *Out of Africa* are all devices to fill in gaps that are difficult to express dramatically.

If a main character doesn't have an equal opponent, the story will feel narrative rather than dramatic. Notice the difference in the scenes in *The Mosquito Coast* when Allie is in conflict with the missionary, from the more narrative scenes of building, making speeches, traveling, arriving, and leaving.

In many films from books, the conflict changes in each act rather than moving from beginning to end. Remember *Out of Africa*, where the conflict in Act One was essentially between Bror and Karen, and the development of the conflict between Denys and Karen took place in Act Two?

When the relational conflict does not move throughout the story, some filmmakers will turn to the theme for cohesiveness. Both *Out of Africa* and *The Mosquito Coast* are thematic pieces where the theme remained the same for all three acts, even though the conflict changes. However, using the theme for cohesiveness reinforces the narrative quality rather than emphasizes the dramatic through-line of the story.

One way I've found of translating novels into scripts is to see if you can reverse the plot and subplot lines. Since the plot line of a novel often revolves around the interior life of the character, this can be made into a smaller subplot line. The more relational subplots can be developed to give a stronger relational through-line.

When I worked on the best-selling novel *Christy*, we ran up against this problem. The main focus of this 500-page novel is Christy's search for identity and her search for God. This theme gets worked out through the story about a girl who comes to the Appalachians in 1912 to teach school. While there, she struggles with her relationships with the schoolchildren, with a minister and doctor, and with an ongoing feud that threatens the lifestyle and lives in the community.

In the novel, the feud is a small subplot that winds its way throughout the story. In reworking the structure of the novel, we brought the feud to the forefront since it gave the most movement to the story. However, in the book, Christy is more an observer than a participant with the feud. We knew she had to be more active in its resolution. To do this, we intersected the feud subplot with the schoolchildren subplot, bringing out several beats in the book that were implied rather than spelled out. We combined scenes and characters from the book, sometimes making Christy the catalyst figure rather than using some minor character from the novel. By bringing Christy into a closer relationship with the feud, we were also able to emphasize the themes of forgiveness, commitment, and finding one's self. *Christy* premiered as a television series in the spring of 1994. As a television series, there will be many conflicts that can be made specific and relational.

Being true to the book often means balancing subplots and plots in a new, more dramatic way. It means bringing out conflicts that are only implied in the book. It means reordering scenes so that the conflict is clear in each act. And it means constantly texturing each scene so that the conflict is a clear through-line throughout the story.

APPLICATION

In the last chapter, we discussed the relationship between the motivation, action, and goal. Now we can add one more element to that through-line—the conflict.

When you define the conflict, try to clearly express the goal of both the antagonist and the protagonist in terms that reveal why they're in conflict. For instance, if I were to map out this through-line with *Witness*, it would look like this:

MOTIVATION	ACTION	GOAL	CONFLICT
John Book is assigned to find a murderer.	He hides out on an Amish farm and tries to find ways	To expose Paul as the murderer.	John *wants* to expose Paul.
Paul is discovered by John.	He tries to kill John, tries to find John, comes after John	To kill John before John exposes him.	Paul *wants* to kill John before he's exposed.

Notice how what John wants is diametrically opposed to what Paul wants. The more clearly you can show this relationship, the stronger the conflict will be.

In working out the conflict, find ways to express it in strong visual and emotional terms. In the Stanislavski method of acting, actors are taught to phrase their superobjective for a role in terms that are actable and dramatic. For instance, if the objective of a scene is to get information, an actor might phrase this goal as "I want to try to get information." That's weak and will not result in a dramatic action. The actor might phrase this goal as "I want to squeeze every ounce of information out of him, no matter what it takes." This will lead to a much stronger scene.

Once you've clearly established the goal for the protagonist and antagonist, and phrased it so that we can clearly see why they are in conflict with each other, begin looking at your other characters. You can shade much of the conflict within scenes by smaller conflicts between supporting characters and the main characters. If your antagonist is a Mafia figure, the chauffeur or the bodyguard might not agree with him in every scene. Perhaps they argue over how to handle another mafioso (one wants to kill him, the other just wants information). Or the dresser and the Mafia boss might disagree about what suit he should wear. Or the wife begins to suspect something that he doesn't want her to know.

In most scripts, each scene presents many opportunities for this kind of texturing.

Then, as you analyze the conflict within your script, ask yourself:

Who is my protagonist and who is my antagonist?
What is their conflict? Is it relational? Societal? Situational? Cosmic? Have I expressed most of the conflict relationally?

How is the conflict expressed? Do I use images and action as well as dialogue to show conflict?

Have I created small conflicts between characters that add extra "punch" to a scene?

Is there one overall conflict that defines the issue of the story? Does it relate to both my storyline and the character spine?

Conflict can be used to express power plays, disagreements, different points of view, different attitudes and philosophies, as well as different overall objectives. Although only one conflict should be the center of the story from beginning to end, remember to use smaller conflicts throughout each scene. These will give your story interest, punch, and dimensionality.

Chapter Eleven

Creating Dimensional Characters

Critics love to pan a film by saying that the character doesn't grow and change. Character **development** is essential to a good story. As a character moves from motivation to goal, something needs to happen in the process. A well-drawn character gains something by their participation in the story, and a story gains something from the character's involvement.

Earlier we spoke about how Rose in *The African Queen* changed the direction of the story because of her personality and willfulness and determination. We see a similar relationship between character and story with Edna in *Places in the Heart*, or Martin and Matt in *Jaws*, or Oskar in *Schindler's List*.

Each of these characters entered the story as dimensional, nonstereotypical characters. Each of them became more dimensional as the story and other characters acted upon them—advising them, teaching them, fighting with them, confronting them, pressuring them, influencing them. Because they were characters who were as big as life, they were capable of developing and being transformed.

We've all seen stereotypical characters who are defined by their physicality. They're one-dimensional. They can usually be described in one or two words: the dumb blonde; the macho detective; the muscle-bound lifeguard; the voluptuous model. Sometimes these characters only have a small role in the story and act as kind of window dressing for the set. But sometimes these types are main characters who limit the film because of their limited dimensions. Well-drawn characters are broader, more fleshed out. We see different sides of them. We understand how they think. We see them act. And we're aware of their emotional make-up through their responses.

Thoughts, actions, and emotions might be defined as the three dimensions of the character.

Most films shortchange one or two of these dimensions. They will emphasize one above the other, creating character types. A character type is a character who is defined by only one category. James Bond is a character type. He's a hero. He's defined by action. We know little about his attitudes (except that he likes to sleep with attractive women). His emotional life is irrelevant and almost nonexistent. You'll never see James Bond cry, show fear, show insecurity, get angry, or be anything other than cool.

We've all seen other types. The weeping widow who is all emotion, the pontificating scholar who is all philosophy, the rescuing hero who is all action.

Each of these categories can be further divided. *Thinking* consists of a character's philosophy, values, attitudes, and point of view. *Acting* consists of actions as well as the decisions that lead to the action. And *emotions* include the emotional make-up of the character as well as emotional responses. With any well-drawn character, one of these categories might be stronger, but each of them will contribute to creating a three-dimensional character.

PHILOSOPHY/ATTITUDES

Philosophy is the most difficult to portray. Characters who are defined too much by their philosophy become abstract, talky, self-indulgent, and usually boring. Yet every dimensional character has a philosophy. Characters do believe in something: perhaps in religion, women's rights, gay liberation, or God, mother, and apple pie. What they believe will begin to affect their actions. A character who believes in gay liberation might march, might be quite vocal about it, or might be a practicing homosexual. That philosophy will begin to find dramatic form in the actions he does.

Characters have *attitudes* toward life. They might be cynical, or positive, or happy-go-lucky, or aggressive. All good characters take a stance toward life. They might have a healthy outlook; they might be neurotic. They might be confident; they might be insecure. They might look at life through rose-colored—or gray-colored—glasses. And their attitudes will have an effect on the actions they take and the way they relate to other characters.

We know the truth about a character through attitude and action rather than through philosophy. When philosophy and action conflict, then we have a hypocrite. If I tell you, "I love humanity" and then proceed to keep everyone at a distance and go out of my way to make other people's lives miserable, obviously my attitude and actions define me and my philosophy is nothing but empty words.

Attitude is more actable than philosophy. It is more easily expressed through action. It's not that difficult to show compassion, or love, or receptivity, or cynicism. But the danger of both philosophy and attitude is the temptation to have the character talk this dimension rather than act it.

DECISIONS/ACTIONS

Action is the lifeblood of drama. In a novel we might focus on feelings and attitudes and beliefs. In drama the focus is action. Action is divided into two parts: the decision to act and the act itself.

When we look at films, we usually see only the action. Yet

it's the decision to act that helps us understand how the character's mind works. The moment of decision—whether to pull the trigger at that moment, whether to say "yes" to an assignment, whether to commit to a relationship—is usually a strong moment of character revelation.

In *Tootsie*, we see a strong comedic scene when Michael has to decide quickly what to do. He is waiting to take Sandy out to dinner. While waiting, he notices a "cute little dress" that looks "just right" for Dorothy in Sandy's closet . He decides to try it on at just the moment that Sandy comes into the bedroom. The moment is open to misinterpretation unless Michael decides and acts quickly:

> SANDY
> (opening door)
> Michael, we don't have to go out to eat.
> We could stay here.

She sees Michael, pants down, and reacts. Michael jumps up, trying to cover himself, and trying to figure out what to say.

> MICHAEL
> Sandy . . . I—I want you!

> SANDY
> (surprised)
> You want me?

> MICHAEL
> (shuffling toward her, pants around ankles,
> arms outstretched)
> I want you!

And we laugh at Michael's quick thinking.

John Book in *Witness* decides *not* to make love with Rachel the night of the barn-raising, and that decision is one of the most powerful moments of the film. Rose, in *The African Queen*, decides to allow Allnutt to sleep under the awning with her, out of the rain, and that decision begins the change in their relationship. Sam Gerard in *The Fugitive* decides what to do and how to do it throughout the film.

Decisions must lead to specific actions. Characters need to be active in a story. It is the job of the main character to drive the story forward with his/her actions. Characters can be active in many different ways. They can search, investigate, uncover, outwit, plan strategy, transform others and themselves, create new environments, manipulate, avenge, and right a wrong. Whatever the action, it's important that it has the ability to drive the story forward, that it takes a number of beats to execute the action, and that it affects the outcome of the story.

There are some stories in which the character begins as a passive character. The story happens to them, and they are pushed in certain directions by the story. In this situation, the main character has to take over at some point. Somewhere, and certainly before the middle of the story, the character needs to begin pushing back. The character needs to begin making the story happen, rather than being at the mercy of the story.

EMOTIONAL LIFE/EMOTIONAL RESPONSES

Emotions often get left out of stories. Or sometimes emotions are limited, consisting of tears and anger and little else. Yet characters have emotional lives that define the character just as their attitudes define them. Their cynical attitude might result in despair, or depression, or in withdrawal from life. They might be sulky, bitter, or angry. A positive attitude might result in a character that smiles or laughs a lot, or is always optimistic, accessible, and reaches out. Or a character might be cool as a result of inaccessible emotions, or hard-hearted, or hostile and vengeful.

Characters' emotional lives define them, and their emotional responses expand this definition. Extraordinary situations bring out extraordinary emotional responses. A character who is usually happy may become angry at an injustice that's been done. A despairing character may be touched by love and whole new emotional responses will emerge. Some films show characters with a very narrow emotional range. Rarely do we know how Karen Blixen feels in *Out of Africa*. At most times, whether the burning of her plantation or her divorce from Bror, she responds rationally. She is more apt to discuss a situation than to cry, get angry, or be afraid. But even her usual response changes under extraordinary circumstances. When Denis Finch-Hatten takes her on her first airplane ride over stunningly beautiful Africa, she gently and tearfully reaches back to clasp his hand in a profound "thank you."

On the opposite extreme, a character such as Tess McGill in *Working Girl* has a very broad emotional palette. Throughout the film, she shows disappointment, anger, determination, anxiety, and joy—her emotional responses pull us into her character and into the film.

Just as many films leave out the beat in the story where the character decides to do an action, they also leave out the beat that shows the emotional response to the action. Films often show powerful actions with a powerful impact. They show the effect these have upon the characters. Sometimes we see someone blown away, but we don't see the emotional response that makes the character understandable. How s/he feels creates sympathy in the audience. It creates identification with the character. Emotions pull us into the story. We experience vicariously the character's journey through their emotions.

THE DIMENSIONAL CHAIN

These dimensions create a dimensional sequence that helps define the character on each level. A character's philosophy cre-

185

ates certain attitudes toward life. These attitudes create decisions that create actions. These actions come out of the character's emotional life, which helps predispose the character to do certain things and not doing others. And as a result of the actions of other characters, the character responds emotionally in a certain way.

THE TRANSFORMATIONAL ARC

In the best of films, at least one of the characters becomes transformed in the process of living out the story. Producers often ask the question, "How does the character change and grow?" They recognize that a strong story with strong characters has the potential to influence and transform the protagonist. Not every film needs a transformational arc, although many of the best films will show at least one of the characters becoming transformed in the process of living out the story. Usually the character transformed is the protagonist. Think about the transformations in *Unforgiven, Fatal Attraction,* or *The Piano.* Sometimes the main character stays the same, but the supporting characters change. In *Back to the Future*, Marty is essentially the same person at the end as at the beginning, but his parents— George and Lorraine McFly—have become very different people.

The transformation of a character can be extreme, moving to an opposite position, or the character can simply move to a moderate position. For instance, a rigid character may have a complete transformation, becoming a spontaneous, life-of-the-party person by the end of the film, or s/he may retain a sense of discipline but might loosen up. We might sketch a transformational arc like this:

BEGINNING POSITION	MODERATE POSITION	EXTREME POSITION
George McFly begins as a nerd, a wimp, controlled by Biff.	If transformation were only moderate, George would have gained confidence but not have completely turned the tables on Biff.	Becomes the opposite—confident, strong, attractive, active, with Biff in his employ.

BEGINNING POSITION	MODERATE POSITION	EXTREME POSITION
Rose in *The African Queen*— tight, rigid, spinsterish.	If Rose had only reached a moderate position, she would have continued a bit rigid, but with moments of spontaneity.	Spontaneous, loving, free, open, married.

Transformational arcs can be subtle. In *The Fugitive,* the transformation of Deputy Sam Gerard is one of attitude. Gradually, over the course of the film, we see him shift from a position of "I don't care whether Richard Kimble is innocent or not" to a position of caring, and respect, as he begins to exert effort to find the one-armed man and capture the villian.

In *Schindler's List*, the shift from materialism to humanity happens very much under the surface, as Oskar Schindler slowly shifts attitudes toward Amon Goethe, attitudes toward the Germans, attitudes toward the Jews, and attitudes toward himself. By the end of the film, something profound has happened as he cries, "I could have done more!

In order for characters to change, they need help. They receive this help from the influence of the story and from the influence of other characters. Sometimes one character is a catalyst for change in other characters. In *Back to the Future*, Marty doesn't need to change, but his parents do. Marty retains the same position throughout the story, but he's the catalyst for extraordinary transformations in his parents. In *Star Wars*, Princess Leia makes few changes throughout the story. She retains her same position, but her influence and her presence create transformations in Han Solo and Luke Skywalker.

In other stories, both characters are transformed. In *The African Queen*, Rose becomes spontaneous and free, and the gin-drinking Allnutt become sober and relational. They both come full circle in their transformation. In *Tootsie*, Michael Dorsey becomes a better man for having been a woman.

It takes time to transform a character. It doesn't happen in a few pages. It usually takes the entire three acts to create a transformation to its opposite. It's a beat-by-beat process, slowly building up the transformation through moments. These moments show changes in many ways. We see the decisions a character makes and how these decisions change throughout the story. We see new emotional responses to a new situation. And we see new actions the character learns to take as a result of the demands of the story and the interactions with the other characters.

To understand the transformation, let's look at the beats that mark Rose's transformation in *The African Queen*. We might map it out this way:

Rose's attitude toward Allnutt and his attitude toward her begin with utter indifference.

ROSE

(Indifferently)
Good morning, Mr. Allnutt.

ALLNUTT

Mornin' Miss . . .

For a moment, Allnutt looks at Rose with utter casualness and indifference.

We can see from this section in the set-up that there is no love lost between the ill-mannered Allnutt and the tight, proper Rose.

When Rose's brother dies and Allnutt returns to check up on them, the relationship has changed already. Rose is grateful for Allnutt's arrival and for his help in burying her brother.

> ALLNUTT
> Tell ya wot. While I'm diggin' the grave, yer get
> yer things together Miss . . .
> Then we can clear out of 'ere.

> ROSE
> Clear out?

> ALLNUTT
> Germans might come back any time.

> ROSE
> Why should they? They left nothing.

> ALLNUTT
> Oh, they'll come back all right.
> Lookin' for *The African Queen* . . .

> ROSE
> Where will we go?

> ALLNUTT
> I thought, Miss, 'ow we might find somewhere
> quiet behind an island! Then we could talk
> about what to do.

                     ROSE
        (a pause, then a quick decision)
      I'll get my things ready.

                  (. . .)
      Thank you, Mr. Allnutt

                ALLNUTT
      You'd do the same for me, Miss.

As he thinks it over, he begins to wonder, literal-mindedly, whether she really would.

The next major beat in their developing relationship happens the first night on the river. Rose is sleeping under the awning and Allnutt in the front of the boat. It begins to rain. To keep dry, Allnutt quietly tries to get under the awning without waking Rose. When she awakens, she thinks the worst of him, and he retreats. Just then, there's an outburst of thunder and lightning. Rose is embarrassed and sorry as she begins to understand the situation.

                   ROSE
     Mr. Allnutt. You may come in out of the rain.

                ALLNUTT
      Sorry I gave you such a turn.

                   ROSE
     That's quite all right, Mr. Allnutt.

He turns away and tries to make himself comfortable . . . Allnutt huddles into the dry space, doing his best not to touch her, yet to stay dry. Upon one elbow she hovers over him, watching him, with a strange, cool, virginal tenderness. Splatterings of rain spray his sleeping face. Gently, but inhumanly, as if he were an ugly little doll, she draws a corner of her rug across him, to protect him.

As they get further down the river, Allnutt realizes that Rose is serious about torpedoing the *Louisa*. When he gets drunk, he calls her a "crazy, psalm-singin', skinny old maid," which only makes her more determined. The next morning, Rose empties all the bottles of Allnutt's booze. Rose is angry . . . and Allnutt tries to change her mood. He shaves and makes light conversation, but it is not until he agrees to her plan of torpedoing *The Louisa* that she stops her silent treatment and becomes kind to him again.

With this beat, they've had a major argument and survived it. Their relationship has changed again. Now they are of one mind, ready to carry out their mission.

By the end of Act One, both Rose and Allnutt have already come a way with their transformation. They have apologized to each other, they have helped each other, and excitement about the adventure is beginning to enliven Rose.

During Act Two, we can see a number of beats showing the changes in their relationship—the first time they kiss, the first time Rose calls Allnutt "dear," the adventures and concerns they share.

After they get past Shona and are safely through the rapids, Allnutt and Rosie celebrate, causing another turning point in their relationship:

ALLNUTT
We made it. We made it!

ROSE
Hip, Hip, Hooray!

ALLNUTT
Oh, we sure put one over on them that time
didn't we, Miss? I didn't believe anyone could.
Well, we showed them!

>   ROSE
>   Hip, Hip, Hooray!

Charlie kisses her. An embarassed silence follows.

>   ROSE
>   Was I handling the boat all right?

>   ALLNUTT
>   Yes, better than all right, Miss.
>   Well, we're running short of fuel.
>   Better put in someplace.

Their plan continues until they get stuck in the rushes and it seems as if all is over for them.

>   ALLNUTT
>   You want to know the truth, don't you?

>   ROSE
>   That's right.

>   ALLNUTT
>   That's right.

>   ROSE
>   Even if we had all our strength we'd never be
>   able to get her off this mud.

>   ALLNUTT
>   Not a chance in this world.

He puts a hand along her cheek. Slowly she realizes, and enhances for us, her only concern with dying.

>   They don't come no better'n you.

And at the very end of the story, when they are about to be executed by the Germans, the transformation is complete:

                    ROSE
Would you hang us together, please?

                  ALLNUTT
Wait a minute, Captain. Would you grant us a last request?

                  CAPTAIN
What is it?

                  ALLNUTT
Marry us?

                  CAPTAIN
What?

                  ALLNUTT
We want to get married. Ship captains can do that, can't they?

                  CAPTAIN
Yeah.

                    ROSE
Why, Charlie, what a lovely idea.

                  CAPTAIN
What kind of craziness is this?

                  ALLNUTT
Oh, come on, Captain. It would only take a minute. And it would mean such a lot to the lady.

CAPTAIN
Very well. If you wish it. Absolutely.

And marry them he does.

CAPTAIN
I now pronounce you man and wife.
Proceed with the execution.

The next moment, the deck heaves upward. There is a rush
of air and a frightful roar.

ALLNUTT
Wot 'appened?

ROSE
We did it, Charlie, we did it!

ALLNUTT
But 'ow?

Rose points to a piece of wreckage floating with the words
"African Queen."

ALLNUTT
Well, I'll be . . . Are you all right, Mrs. Allnutt?

ROSE
Simply wonderful. And you, Mr. Allnutt?

ALLNUTT
Pretty good for an old married man.

ROSE
I'm all turned 'round, Charlie. Which way is
the south shore?

ALLNUTT
The way we're swimming, old girl.

Notice how *The African Queen* takes its time with the beats of the transformation. Nothing happens too quickly. Changes occur as each character confronts the rigors of the situation, as their intentions collide and eventually join together, and from their need of each other to accomplish their goal. Each character feels the influence of the other and responds through new actions and new emotions. The people they were at the beginning of the story are not the people they become.

The African Queen is an excellent example of story influencing character and character influencing story. It's clear and consistent and realistic. As a result, we are involved in the beat-by-beat changes in Rose and Allnutt.

PROBLEMS IN CREATING THE DIMENSIONAL CHARACTER

Sometime ago, I worked with a writer who had written one of the hit films of 1985. He was working on another script that was very complex, very difficult, and contained a woman protagonist who was described as a "leggy, beautiful blonde." As I worked on the script, it was readily apparent that he had created a stereotype with none of the dimensionality or originality of his male charcters. This surprised me since I knew him to be an excellent writer, as well as a happily married liberated male with a successful working wife.

When he arrived at the meeting, before I even had an opportunity to begin talking about his female protagonist, he immediately began talking about his frustration with this character. He simply couldn't get her to work. And he pleaded with me to believe that he "wasn't that kind of man." He emphasized that he saw women as dimensional and whole people, that he loved his wife, and that some of his best friends were women. Nevertheless, he couldn't get this woman character to come to life and he assured me that he was capable of writing better characters.

As we began working with her, I told him that he had painted himself into a corner with his description of her. Once he physically described her in a stereotypical way, there was no way that his character could break out of it.

I suggested that we begin by changing the description of her. Instead of describing her for her beauty, we tried to approach her in the same way that he approached his male characters. They were described by what they wore, by their integrity (or lack of it), by their attitudes, and by their looks of despair or hope on their faces. Once he found a more realistic description of her, the character became more dimensional.

Creating dimensional characters is not easy. There are many traps and pitfalls for the writer. Sometimes writers give in to the temptation to look to other films, rather than to life, for the source of their characters. I have read more than one script that describes a character as a "Harrison Ford type as he appeared in *Raiders of the Lost Ark*" or "a James Bond type as played by Roger Moore."

Sometimes writers leave out one aspect of their characters—such as philosophy or emotional response—because it's not as overt or easily recognizable as action. The films they see often emphasize one element above another, which leads them to think that other dimensions aren't important.

Creating dimensional characters demands observance of real life. The best writers seem to be constantly noticing small details and character traits and listening for character rhythms. They make a commitment to moving beyond stereotypes and expanding their own understanding of people. And they have a respect for their characters, giving them freedom to find a broad range of thoughts, actions, and emotions.

APPLICATION

When reworking a character, it's often helpful to begin with the transformational arc. Begin by looking at the skills and characteristics your main character needs in order to attain the objective. For instance, Rose in *The African Queen* will need to acquire spontaneity, resourcefulness, courage, determination, and love to become the woman at the end of the story. Now look at where your character starts. Work out which of those characteristics your character will have at the beginning of the story and which will need to be acquired as the story proceeds.

Now think through how the character will acquire those changes. What will the story demand? How will other characters help your main character achieve the goal?

Now ask yourself: Is there evidence within this story of the philosophy of your character? Is this expressed through actions rather than through talk? Do we clearly see your character's attitudes? Do we know how s/he feels about others and feels about the situation? Do these attitudes lead to certain actions?

If you want your character to be sympathetic, then check emotional responses and ways that you show us the character's emotional make-up. Try to broaden the emotional palette of your character. Some psychologists say that emotions fall into the categories of mad, sad, glad, and scared. Within each of these categories, there are other emotions such as rage, being peeved, frustrated or irritated, being delighted, ecstatic, or gleeful, and being frozen with fear or having an adrenalin rush because of the danger of the situation. Find ways to expand your characters' emotions beyond the usual fear, anger, and passion.

Look at the actions of your characters. Are they playing an active or passive role in the story? Do their actions help move the story as well as help define them as characters? Some characters like to putter. Others knit, read, or collect small objects. Some characters have nervous habits. Others have idiosyncrasies such as "manicuring" everything they come in contact with, whether removing dust or polishing doorknobs or filing nails.

All of these action details will help expand and reveal your characters while still focusing on the necessary actions to advance the story.

As you look through the dimensions and transformations in your script, ask yourself:

Have I gotten stuck in stereotypes? Have I defined certain characters through one dimension rather than creating three-dimensional characters?

What is the transformational arc of my protagonist? Have I given my character(s) enough time to change? Is the change credible?

What are the influences upon my main characters that help them change? Is there a catalyst character? Is there a love relationship? Does the story force changes in my character?

Do we clearly see, through images and action, how the influence of the story and other characters create the transformation? Does the transformation help me express both my theme and my story?

Paying attention to dimensionality and transformation will help you create characters that audiences are not likely to forget. And by emphasizing these elements, you will also enhance identification and commercial viability.

Chapter Twelve

Character Functions

There are many scripts that seem muddy, bogged down, weighty. Sometimes this is a story problem. Sometimes the story is confused, inconsistent, unstructured. Often it's a character problem. There are simply too many characters. We don't know what they're doing there. We might like them, but they seem unnecessary to the unfolding action. Characters begin to run into each other or to confuse the story. We don't know where to put our focus or who to follow.

In a two- to three-hour film, there are only a certain amount of characters we can absorb. Too many overwhelm us, like watching a three-ring circus. We simply don't know where to look. Generally, a film can only support six or seven main characters. In most cases, we see three to five. This might include the protagonist, the love interest, and perhaps one or two supporting characters. In an ensemble piece, like *The Big Chill*, *Diner, St. Elmo's Fire, The Breakfast Club,* or *The Magnificent Seven*, you will usually see five to seven characters. Rarely will you see more.

Of course, that leads to the question, "Where to cut?" You probably have your your favorite characters, characters who are unique and memorable. Unfortunately, "favorite" is not a workable criteria. Generally, when it comes to cutting characters, it becomes essential to look at **character functions.**

Every character in a film should have an essential role to play. They contribute something specific to the production. They might give a clue or information to a detective in a mystery, or be the love interest, or add wisdom or depth to the story, or be a character whose function it is to add stature to a main character (a bodyguard, assistant, etc.). But everyone has a reason for being in the story.

Many characters will perform more than one function. There might be a character who is the love interest, a catalyst and a confidante. However, in most cases, there will not be several characters performing the same function. If several characters do the same function, the effect of each character will be dissipated. Repeating the same type of character means that the writer will not have sufficient time to dimensionalize any one character.

We might divide character functions into five categories: main characters, supporting characters, characters who add dimension, thematic characters, and mass-and-weight characters.

MAIN CHARACTERS

The main characters "do" the action. They're the ones responsible for moving the story along. They are the focus of the film. They provide the main conflict and are sufficiently interesting to keep us intrigued for two or three hours.

The main character is the protagonist. This is who the story is about. This is the person who we're expected to follow, to root for, to empathize with, to care about. Almost always it's a positive figure. It's the hero of the story, like James Bond, Luke Skywalker, Ridley in *Aliens*, Oskar Schindler. This does not mean that the character is perfect or without flaws. Sometimes we might get angry at the protagonist. There might be certain traits that we dislike, but the protagonist commands our attention. A protagonist is eminently watchable.

Occasionally, a protagonist is a type of negative character. *Prizzi's Honor, Amadeus,* and *Gone With the Wind* all show us characters who are not necessarily sympathetic or empathetic. Nevertheless, they involve us. We see the story from their point of view.

Every protagonist needs to be opposed by someone to provide dramatic conflict. This figure is the antagonist. Usually the antagonist is the person who stands against the hero. Mozart was the antagonist for Salieri; Darth Vader stood against Luke Skywalker; Paul Schaeffer opposed John Book.

Sometimes the antagonist is a combination of people. It might be the ghosts in *Ghostbusters* or the townspeople in *Jaws*. In these cases, the antagonist might be a group of supporting characters whose function it is to keep the protagonist from achieving the goal.

The protagonist often has a *love* interest. This character serves to dimensionalize and deepen the main character.

In *Tootsie*, Julie's vulnerability, beauty, relationship with her child, and femininity all served to move Michael from the insensitive macho to sensitive friend. And Michael's particular perspective forced a change in Julie's life.

SUPPORTING ROLES

Characters cannot get through the story alone. They need help and support in accomplishing their goals. They need supporting characters to stand with them and to stand against them—people who give information, who listen, advise, push or pull them, force them to make decisions, confront them, invigorate them.

One function of a supporting character is as a confidante. We often find the confidante in plays, particularly in those delightful English comedies of the 1700s in which the maid is often the person to whom our heroine tells her deepest, darkest secrets. Our heroine confides in the confidante, telling her who she loves, her fears about their imminent meeting, her jealousies, and her concerns. She weeps with her, laughs with her, and calls upon her for help in planning a strategy that will bring her into the arms of her own true love.

In films, the confidante is often a much less interesting character. It does not need to be so, but, unfortunately, the confidante is usually thought of as the character in whom the protagonist confides, rather than reveals himself/herself to. This causes a great deal of talkiness, which substitutes for good drama.

Often, the confidante is used as an excuse for giving information to an audience. As a result, scenes with a confidante often get bogged down, filled with long expository speeches, and used as an opportunity to tell everything that seems difficult to show dramatically.

But the confidante need not be dull. Think of the confidante as the person to whom the protagonist reveals herself rather than talks to. This is a trustworthy character in whose presence the protagonist can be him/herself. Instead of talking and listening, the confidante can provide an opportunity for the protagonist to cry, or laugh, or be vulnerable, thus revealing other dimensions of character.

Sometimes the confidante is a partner, even another protagonist. In *Butch Cassidy and the Sundance Kid*, or *48 Hours,* or *Lethal Weapon*, the partners are able to be confidantes for each other. In many television series, partners and work associates function as confidantes when necessary, even though their main function may be to move the action forward. (Notice the confidante figures of The Commander and Major Kira in "Deep Space Nine," Dr. Mark Sloane and his detective son in "Diagnosis: Murder," or Jessica's confidante relationship with some of her relatives in "Murder She Wrote.")

Another important character function is the catalyst character. These are the people who provide a piece of information or cause an event to happen that pushes the protagonist into action. In *Witness*, Samuel is a catalyst figure. He's the character who sees the murder and reports it to John Book. As a result, John Book can get on with his job.

In *Tootsie,* Sandy is a catalyst figure since it's Sandy who tells Michael Dorsey about the soap-opera job.

Catalyst figures can be minor figures. In *The Fugitive,* the man on the bus who starts to cough, and then stabs the guard, is a catalyst for the accident, and, therefore, Richard Kimble's escape.

Sometimes a catalyst figure delivers a clue that sends the detective on a different track, thereby solving the crime.

Sometimes a catalyst figure forces a transformation in the protagonist. In this case, the catalyst might be a therapist, parent, or friend who confronts the protagonist, pushing for change. Or a catalyst might be the police who arrests the protagonist, pushing for change. Or a catalyst might be the police who arrest the protagonist, or the judge who gives a sentence that forces the protagonist to change his ways.

Almost every story has catalyst figures. The protagonist cannot do it alone. Every protagonist needs help in getting and keeping the story moving.

When creating catalyst figures, it's important to make them active so that they catapult the story forward through action, not dialogue.

CHARACTERS WHO ADD OTHER DIMENSIONS

If a story were simply linear, with the protagonist achieving a goal with just a little help from a catalyst or two, the film would begin to lose your interest. There are always some characters who provide dimensionality for the story and for the main characters. This does not necessarily mean that the character is dimensional, but that the film becomes more dimensionalized because of the character's presence.

We've all seen serious films with one funny character who provides the humor. This character's function is to bring comic relief, to lighten up the story, to give the audience an opportunity to release tension. If you've read much Shakespeare, you might remember that even in the most serious stories, there's usually some character who makes us laugh. The obvious example, of course, is Falstaff in *King Henry IV, Parts I and II*. In Shakespeare's tragedies, there's the blabbering porter in *Macbeth*, the Nurse in *Romeo and Juliet*, and the Fool in *King Lear*.

Many films use comic-relief characters. In *Star Wars*, we get humor from R2D2 and C3PO, who is always complaining "we're doomed," and from Chewabacca, who the Princess Leia calls "a hairy carpet."

Even in comedies, the humor is often focused on a supporting character who makes us laugh, such as the nerd in *Ghostbusters* or Professor Brown in *Back to the Future*.

In many stories, we see a character who contrasts with the protagonist. In *Witness,* Daniel is a *contrasting character* to John Book. Perhaps you remember the scene when Rachel and her suitor sit on the porch swing, tensely drinking lemonade and having little to say to each other. Contrast that scene with Rachel and John dancing in the barn, or John making jokes over morning coffee, or the passion between Rachel and John at the beginning of Act Three. Daniel's presence throws John's character into high relief, making us more aware of certain characteristics of John and further dimensionalizing him.

In an early draft of *Witness*, John's sister, Elaine, serves as a contrasting character to Rachel. She's drawn as undisciplined, defensive, and a messy housekeeper. When Rachel stays at her home, there's a long scene when Rachel cleans up the house with the help of the children, thereby contrasting her neat, disciplined ways with Elaine's sense of being overwhelmed by the task.

In *Tootsie,* we see some contrasts between Sandy and Julie, and Michael and Ron, particularly since Michael treats Sandy much like Ron treats Julie. We see a contrast between Sandy's attitude toward Dorothy Michaels (she doesn't like her) and Julie's attitude toward her (she wants to be best friends). The contrast between Sandy and Julie helps expand the theme of love and friendship and helps expand the feminine images that serve to dimensionalize and contrast with Dorothy.

The contrasting characters help us see the main characters more clearly because of differences between them. They expand the depth of the story. Like an artist's palette, they add texture and focus, clarifying certain subtle character traits.

THEMATIC CHARACTERS

There are a number of characters who serve to convey and express the theme of a film. Although one or two of these characters might be found in any kind of film—whether action-adventure, mystery, comedy, or drama—a film that is theme-oriented, such as *Gone With the Wind, Amadeus, or Tootsie* might contain many of these characters. In these films, the filmmaker has something definite s/he wants to say. The driving force behind making the film is not so much fascination with the story or characters, but fascination with an idea. It might be about the nature of love and friendship in *Tootsie*, about mediocrity and genius in *Amadeus*, or about the world of the South that is *Gone With the Wind*. But the theme is the impetus for the story.

To communicate a theme, a filmmaker turns to characters for help. In many thematically complex stories, one character is the balance character, who makes sure that the theme is not misrepresented or misinterpreted.

Some films demand this balance character because they leave themselves open for misinterpretation. Films that deal with gay or lesbian issues sometimes need to balance their gay characters with some strong heterosexual roles. Otherwise the film might be in danger of being misinterpreted as being too myopic in its perspective. In a film like *Desert Hearts, Longtime Companion,* or *Philadelphia*, these balance characters can help the story appeal to a broader audience.

Films in which minorities play important negative roles

need to be balanced by positive role models. *The Year of the Dragon* was severely criticized for its portrayals of Asians because it didn't have positive Asian characters. The plot of *Soul Man*, about a white person posing as a black in order to get a scholarship, was open to misinterpretation. Even *The Color Purple* was criticized for its one-dimensional male figures because it seemed to give an unbalanced picture of black men.

The balance in any of these films can usually be maintained by showing one character who presents the other side. In *The Color Purple*, one or two positive and dimensional black men could have balanced out the portrait of Mr. and Harpo. A positive minority character can balance the minority villain. Without this character, films can be open to misunderstanding or worse: to protests, angry letters, and perhaps an unreleasable film.

Some thematic characters dimensionalize the theme by showing different points of view, thereby helping communicate the complexity of the idea. We might call these characters the "voice of . . . " character. For instance, in *Witness,* Eli is the "voice of" Amish nonviolence as he talks to Samuel about the problems and evils of violence. In *Unforgiven*, Will Munny, through reaction, not dialogue, carries the voice of nonviolence as he reacts to the Scofield Kid's excitement over being a gunslinger. And in *Schindler's List,* Izthak Stern is a "Voice of Clarity and Insight" communicating the clearest perception of good and evil.

It's important not to take the "voice of . . . " character too literally. These are not meant to be talky characters. Instead they convey their idea through attitude, action, and—occasionally—dialogue.

Another character often used to communicate the theme is the writer's point-of-view character. Here the writer chooses a particular character to communicate what s/he wants to say in the story. In a sense, this character is the writer's alter ego. In *Star Wars*, this character is probably Obi-Wan-Kenobi or, in the second film of the trilogy, *The Empire Strikes Back*, Yoda. Any philosophy or attitude that the writer wants to convey can easily be given through either of these characters.

It's not always important for the audience to know who the writer's point-of-view character is. However, if you as the writer have something specific that you want to get across in your script, then choose a character who can do this for you. It will need to be a character you identify with, and it will probably need to be a supporting character. If you had certain attitudes you wanted to communicate about sharks, then you would choose Matt in *Jaws*. In *Schindler's List,* the writer's point-of-view character is probably Stern. In *Amadeus* it's probably the priest who hears Salieri's confession.

Sometimes this particular character becomes essential to the story that's being told, because the story is dependent on a clear message being conveyed from the writer to the audience. If you are working with controversial material where there's not a clear right or wrong, then there needs to be some help given to the audience so that they know how to think through the message in order to gain some insight into a complex story.

Some time ago, I worked on a Movie-of-the-Week about the problems of gun control. This is a controversial subject with very few clear answers. On the one hand, we live in a violent society. Many citizens have had the experience of being mugged, raped, or robbed and wished that they had had a gun to protect themselves. Some have had guns, only to kill a family member by mistake, or been force to live with the guilt of killing another human being, albeit a burglar. So there are no easy answers.

When the writers wrote a script about this problem, they wanted to show several different points-of-view without its being a talky, message-oriented film. At the same time, they risked not giving any insight as a result of being unbiased.

To solve this problem, we discussed their own personal point-of-view and tried to clarify exactly what they believed about this subject. We phrased the point of view as "When society doesn't solve their problems, individuals are left trying to solve the problem of violence on an individual level. No matter what the individual does, it will not give the individual a clear answer because it must be solved on the social level."

Once they agreed on this statement, we chose a minor character to convey this viewpoint. If audiences were looking for insight, they could find it somewhere in the story. Otherwise they were in danger of seeing the film as a description of a situation, without clear answers.

Sometimes a screenplay deals with "incredible" material such as the supernatural, UFOs, psychics, reincarnation, etc. In many cases, most of the audience will not believe in this philosophy. They may be skeptics. To make this material work, it's important to choose a character who represents the audience's point-of-view. Perhaps it's a skeptic, who says everything that the audience is thinking at the beginning of the story. As the skeptical character changes and becomes more convinced during the course of the story, the audience skeptics will also be carried along by the situation and change their attitudes. This does not necessarily mean that the story has made true believers of the audience, but that it has suspended their disbelief for the course of the film so that they can identify with the character and become involved as the story unfolds.

This was done particularly well with the miniseries of Shirley MacLaine's best-seller, *Out on a Limb*. The story dealt with her spiritual quest into past lives and reincarnation—not exactly a subject for mass audiences. Yet, there were plenty of audience point-of-view characters—ranging from Jerry the lover to Bella Abzug to Shirley herself—for all the skeptics in the audience. For true believers, there was the character of David, some of the Peruvians, and the transformed Shirley. No matter what side you were on, there was somebody you could identify with and somebody who represented your belief.

MASS-AND-WEIGHT CHARACTERS

Then there are small supporting roles that provide mass and weight to demonstrate the prestige, power, or stature of the protagonist or antagonist. The bodyguards, secretaries, assistants, right-hand men, and gal Fridays that surround powerful men and women all help us understand who's important. The amount of mass and weight you need will depend very much on what's necessary to communicate power.

Most powerful men, particularly if villains, will surround themselves with one or two bodyguards, perhaps a chauffeur, maybe even an assistant. But be careful. Add too many people and you'll have clutter, not mass. Too few will diminish power. If you need a lot of mass, you can often add another character function to a character. For instance, you might make the bodyguard also a confidante figure. Or gal Fridays might be a catalyst figure who propels the story toward its conclusion.

Sometimes it's necessary to focus on particular characters within this mass. This can be accomplished by creating certain immediately recognizable characteristics for one or two characters and leaving the other characters in the background as nameless, faceless, somewhat shadowy masses. Sometimes one character stands out because that character is a different size, has a different ethnic background, or has some other unique characteristic.

In many stories, characters fulfill more than one function. No matter how many functions, it's essential that they have a place in the story and a contribution to make to the story. Clarifying a character function can bring a story into focus. It can save characters who might seem unnecessary. It can help determine who to cut. It has saved many scripts that seemed muddy and confused and were refocused through clear character functions.

PROBLEMS WITH CHARACTER FUNCTIONS

When *The Cotton Club* came out in the early 1980s, one reviewer mentioned that there were "too many" characters. He couldn't differentiate them and couldn't remember if he had met them before.

In any large film, this is a problem. The film needs many characters, yet the audience needs to know who's important and what these key characters are offering to the story. The writer's job is to help the audience stay focused while creating a background of characters to give texture to the film.

Think about how much you need to learn in the first twenty minutes of a film. Characters need to be introduced. You usually need to learn their names, be able to quickly identify them by sight, and have a sense of what each character is contributing to the story.

During the writing and rewriting process, establishing story focus and clarifying character functions is mainly a matter of cutting and combining and honing characters. Once the film goes into production, this becomes a casting problem.

Films like the *Police Academy* films, *Platoon, The Deer Hunter,* or *Gandhi* need a lot of characters. Main characters need to be set against background characters who establish the environment of the film. Usually, the problems are solved in casting through careful differentiation of characters.

The fastest way to remember a character is through ethnic type. Probably weight and height come next. Voice and style of clothes also help audiences build details as they separate one character from another. In *Platoon* and the *Police Academy* films, you saw all of these used. *Platoon* also differentiated characters through quickly establishing the memorable scarred face of Barnes, and through the use of tattoos and attitudes and movement.

But casting cannot solve all the problems and certainly can do little to help if character functions have not been clarified by the writer. In all these films, the writer paid attention to what each character was contributing to the story. Each writer oriented us fairly quickly to what the story was about, who was important, why they were important, and who we were to watch most closely in order to stay with the story.

APPLICATION

It's always difficult to cut or change characters that a writer loves. Yet the job of rewriting means, at times, being ruthless. When doing a rewrite to clarify character functions, often a favorite character will need to be cut or combined with another character.

As you begin the rewrite, look through the characters in your script and clarify the major functions within the script. Do we know who the major character is? Is your protagonist driving the action? Does he or she achieve the climax of the story?

If there are several protagonists, make sure that it's either an equal-partnership story or that one protagonist is taking a bit more focus. In *Ghostbusters*, Dr. Peter Venkman (Bill Murray) is more in focus. In *Star Wars*, Luke Skywalker takes a bit more focus than Han Solo or even Princess Leia. In *Jaws,* Martin is more in focus than Quint or Matt.

Identify your antagonist. Who opposes your protagonist? If it's several characters or situations, be clear which is the major one and make sure that the antagonist is moving throughout the script.

Do you have a confidante? If so, are the confidante scenes overly talky or have you found ways to reveal and show, rather than tell?

Do you have several characters with the same function? If so, cut or combine characters.

Are you missing a function? Perhaps you need another catalyst figure, or perhaps your audience will have trouble understanding the theme without a thematic character.

Is your protagonist receiving help along the way from supporting characters? Are they really supporting your character or simply hanging around?

As a writer, do you have a character who carries your personal point-of-view? If so, have you kept the character active and dramatic rather than talky? Does your point-of-view give insight to the story, or is it simply a message you've been trying to get across and thought you'd sneak it in here?

Are you dealing with material open to misinterpretation? If so, have you included at least one balance character to protect yourself?

Is there humor in your film? Does one character carry the comic relief? Do you use humor to release tension, or to lighten up the material, or to create greater audience enjoyment?

Count how many characters are taking focus throughout the story. If we need to identify and keep track of more than seven, begin finding places to cut so that we can easily follow the story and the various character through-lines.

As you do a checklist of functions, ask yourself:

Are my protagonist and antagonist clear? If there are several antagonists, is one more in focus than others?

Who are my supporting characters? How do they contribute to the story? If I have thematic characters, have I given them other functions so that they aren't merely "message" characters?

Are there catalyst characters who help move the action?

Does every character have a function in my story? If I have several characters with the same function, can I combine characters? Are there any functions missing that my story needs?

Many films have failed at the box office because they had too many characters without clear story functions. Great scripts are clean, clear, and easy to follow. Characters take focus to perform a function, and each character has a reason to be in the story.

Part Four

A Case Study

Chapter Thirteen

On the Road to the Academy Award: A Case Study of the Rewrite of *Witness*

Virtually every script encounters many obstacles on the road from writing to selling to filming. The average for good experienced writers with a workable script and good contacts seems to be about five years. For new writers, it's usually longer. Statistically, the first—and even the second—script rarely sells. Most writers need about five to ten scripts to learn the craft well. Once a writer has learned the craft and created the several good "calling cards" that show the ability to write, one still needs to know how to sell the script. This means having (and finding) good contacts, learning to "take a meeting" (even learning "to do lunch"), and learning a good attitude. Everybody pays their dues many times over in the filmmaking business. The most successful people are willing to pay those dues, are talented, and very, very patient.

Witness is no exception. It took approximately five years from the writing of the script to the release of the film. And it traveled a circuitous route, with the evolution of the story going back to the early 1970s.

THE BACKGROUND

The success of *Witness* was dependent on the ideas of three accomplished writers. Pamela Wallace, Earl Wallace and William Kelley received story credit, and the screenplay was written by Earl Wallace and William Kelley.

Pamela Wallace had four published novels to her credit when she saw an article in the *Los Angeles Times* that intrigued her. It told of an incident where teenage boys threw rocks at an Amish carriage and killed an Amish baby. From this article, she created a proposal for a novel about an Amish woman who comes to Los Angeles and witnesses a murder. The proposal didn't sell, but Earl thought it would make a good screenplay. When the Writers Guild went on strike in 1980, Pamela suggested that they write a spec script on this story.

Earl was already a successful screenwriter, working as story editor on both "Gunsmoke" and "How the West Was Won" and as a staff writer on "The Winds of War" miniseries. Using Pamela's book proposal as a basic outline, he spent about six weeks writing the first draft. Upon completing the draft, he felt that there were similarities to a story that William Kelley had written for "How the West Was Won." He decided to call Bill and suggested they collaborate.

Like Pamela, William Kelley was interested in the Amish. He had studied for the priesthood at an Augustinian seminary near Lancaster County, Pennsylvania, where he had ample opportunity to observe the Amish. He was impressed by their honesty, their directness, and their stand on nonviolence. They were excellent businessmen, excellent carpenters, and good judges of horseflesh. He became familiar with their way of life and their character.

Some years after leaving seminary, he became a novelist, publishing three novels before turning to television writing.

In 1972, he sold an idea to ABC for a two-hour series pilot called "Jedidiah." The story was about an Amish bishop who drives by horse and buggy from Lancaster, Pennsylvania, to set up a new Amish community in Lancaster, California. ABC commissioned the script, but did not put it into production.

Bill then took this idea and wrote a "Gunsmoke" episode in 1975 called *The Pig Man*. This story was about an Amish-type community that he called the Simonites. Richter, a gunslinger, defends a Simonite girl from an assault by four brothers. In the process, he kills one of the brothers and is wounded. He's taken to the Simonite community (called the Bruderhof) to recover. There he falls in love.

"Gunsmoke" was cancelled before the story was filmed. However, the producer of "Gunsmoke," John Mantley, soon became the producer of the miniseries "How the West was Won." He asked Bill to redo his story, making it one of the main storylines for the miniseries. With some small changes in character, the storyline was incorporated and finally played on television in 1977.

Since Earl and Bill had worked together on both "Gunsmoke" and "How the West Was Won," they knew each other, were both experienced writers, and were both in tune with the idea. The collaboration proved to be an excellent match.

SELLING THE SCRIPT

With the completion of the script, a producer, Edward Feldman, optioned the script for $22,000. However, this option did not mean that it would be produced. Since Feldman had a first-refusal deal with Twentieth Century-Fox, he took the script to them. They turned it down.

Then he gave it to Harrison Ford to read. He expressed interest in doing the project. With his interest, Paramount Studios decided to buy the script.

At this point, the creative team of Ed Feldman, his development executive, David Bombyk, and writers Bill Kelley and Earl Wallace began interviewing directors. They were interested in Peter Weir, but he was unavailable since he was slated to direct *The Mosquito Coast*. Several others were considered, but none seemed right for the project. One said that he thought that the script would work better "with a funny ending." Another didn't have any ideas about an approach to the script, except that he'd "figure it out later." Peter Weir then became available because the production of *The Mosquito Coast* was pushed back another year. After an initial meeting with Peter, everyone agreed to the choice. Peter had a specific point of view to bring to the script. He was interested in the pacifism of the story and wanted to get across the theme of nonviolence. He saw many ways of building up the cultural clash between the Amish and the police. And he appreciated how this situation was "peculiarly American." It seemed to be a very good match.

Shortly afterward Alexander Godonov was chosen for the role of Daniel Hochstetler. After looking at a number of actresses for the part of Rachel, they sought out Kelly McGillis, who had last been seen in *Reuben*, and who was currently waitressing in Brooklyn while waiting for another film.

The creative team seemed particulary well-balanced. All were experienced, and each had a particular perspective to offer the film. Ed Feldman had produced a number of films and television shows, including *The Other Side of the Mountain (Parts One* and *Two), Save the Tiger, The Last Married Couple In America,* and *The Golden Child*. He had a background in public relations and had insights into "what makes it commercial."

Peter Weir was particularly interested in the theme. He had something that he wanted to say with the film about nonviolence, and he wanted to create a mood through a lyrical approach to the script.

Bill's background in the seminary oriented him to the spiritual dimension of the piece and a love and understanding of the Amish. Earl, with his background as a story editor, was particularly plot-oriented. And co-producer David Bombyk focused on the consistency, the story spine, and making sure that everything came together like it needed to.

Paramount Studios was interested in the project, since they

believed that *Witness* would be nominated for Best Original Screenplay and Best Director, with the possibility of other nominations.

Now the real process of rewriting began.

CHANGES IN THE POINT-OF-VIEW

In the original book proposal by Pamela, and in the original drafts of *Witness*, the story belongs to Rachel more than to John. In the early drafts, many of the emotional moments are Rachel's. Her backstory is brought out more clearly in Act One, as we learn that the Amish way is to marry within a year after the death of a spouse, but Rachel wants more time. She decides to go visit her sister in Baltimore in order to decide whether to marry Daniel and to resolve some of her confusion about the Amish way of life.

In the early drafts, Rachel is the focus of the first subplot turning point. As she cares for John, she feels drawn to him. The script describes a woman struggling with an erotic attraction to John. She's confused by the physicality of the situation. As the story develops further, we see Rachel clearly falling in love with John. At the second turning point, Rachel actually confronts John, asking him to stay. This love scene, which was particularly strong in the early drafts, was the subject of much discussion. Earl wanted to show John and Rachel making love. Bill wanted to show just a passionate kiss. Peter agreed on the kiss but didn't want it to be passionate. The entire love scene was filmed, but only the kiss remained after editing.

During rewriting, the story focused more on John Book and became more his story. At the first turning point of the film, although we see some response from Rachel, the camera focuses more on John's reaction when he realizes that Rachel has stayed up all night to care for him. At the second turning point, there's only one line about staying or leaving and the issue is never really confronted.

Other changes in the point-of-view were made to soften the relationship between John and Rachel. In some of the early drafts, Rachel is much more feisty and more confrontive. Some of these interchanges were filmed, but they were not workable since they made Rachel irritating and bossy.

Some scenes were added to soften their relationship. The dance scene was added, as was the breakfast scene in Act Two. These balanced the cuts in Act One, while giving extra beats to the development of their relationship in Act Two.

These changes in the point-of-view refocused the film toward John Book. But they also served to create a stronger relational line between John and Rachel.

SCENES THAT WERE CUT

To a great extent, rewriting is a process of balancing a film. Sometimes that means cutting some of the best scenes. Some of these cuts take place in the rewriting process, some of them take place during editing.

One of Bill's favorite scenes took place between Rachel and John's sister Elaine. In the film, we see a scene where Rachel stays with Elaine overnight so that John can continue to question Samuel the next morning. In the script, Rachel gets up the next morning and begins cleaning the house (which desperately needs it). Elaine gets furious, seeing her actions as a criticism of her housekeeping abilities.

The scene was well-written. It had conflict. It contrasted with Rachel and Elaine. It added character dimensions to both Rachel and Elaine. But it also added little to the story. Since the story needed to move quickly to Act Two, this was one scene that could be cut without jeopardizing the storyline.

Substantial cutting also took place around John's backstory. When we watch the film, we're aware that John Book is a detective assigned to investigate a murder. We know that the man who was killed (Zenovich) was an undercover police officer. We know that John believes that the murderer is one of the men on the street, possibly Coalmine, who hangs out at the Happy Valley Bar.

The backstory, which was worked out in rewriting and then cut, was much more complex than this. In one draft of the script, we learn a great deal of additional information. We learn that John's job on the police force is to investigate police corruption, which makes him unpopular with other police officers. We learn that he's a crusader. We discover that John's partner, Carter, was supposed to meet Zenovich, but arrived late, thereby he feels as if his irresponsibility might have contributed to the murder.

There was also additional information about the PCP and how it contributed to the murder. In one of the discussions, who confiscated the PCP, when, and the ways that Paul and McFee and Fergie were involved were all sketched out. Most of this also was cut in editing.

Most of the cutting, particularly in Act One, was designed to move the story to the Amish farm as quickly as possible. Any information that seemed merely expository, any details that didn't seem necessary to set up and pay off the story, were cut. Any scenes that were character revelation scenes, but were not contributing to the story, were cut. In spite of many rich details in these scenes, the decision was made by Peter Weir and editor Thom Noble that it was essential to set up the story quickly so that the story development at the Amish farm could begin.

SCENES THAT WERE CHANGED

Many scenes were changed because of the influence of the actors. Peter and Harrison discussed each scene, and would often go off by themselves and "cook up" ideas that would add to a scene, or texture a scene differently. Peter suggested the dance scene in Act Two, but Harrison chose the song and expanded upon the idea. Harrison, who had tried a number of times to get cast in the Maxwell House commercial, added the Maxwell House line, "Good coffee, honey," The line worked, creating more contrast between the Amish life and the world of the city and advertising.

The barn-raising scene had a number of changes between writing and filming. Originally, the barn-raising sequence had cutaways to a scene of Carter being tortured and killed. Peter wanted to cut the Carter scene, believing that the emotional impact would be greater if we found out about his death at the same time as John Book. And he wanted to play the barn-raising scene as one long scene. To bring out the lyricism of the scene, he reduced the amount of conflict between John, Rachel, and Daniel.

Originally, the screenplay retained the incident from the *Los Angeles Times* newspaper article about punks killing an Amish baby. In one draft, this was changed to a truck crashing into the Amish carriage. For the film, punks confront the Amish and are punched out by John Book.

Act Three went through considerable changes, many of them after arriving in Lancaster County to begin filming.

In the film, three men come after John: Paul Schaeffer, McFee, and Fergie. Peter felt that he could create more tension by only having McFee arrive. He suggested that Fergie could have been killed during the murder of Carter, thereby justifying why he wasn't there. Bill felt that it was absolutely essential that all three men were there, since one man would not present as great a threat to John. After considerable discussion, it was agreed—there would be three men.

But how were they to be killed? In an early draft, McFee was killed by an ornery mule. This was vetoed by Peter, who asked, "How are you going to get a mule to kick on cue?" Peter began looking at Amish farms and came up with the inspired idea to use a silo for the murder scene. This was easier said than done, since it was impossible to film in a silo, and since silos did not work by opening a door and flooding them with grain. Believing that few audience members would understand the workings of an Amish silo, the group agreed on the solution and a silo was constructed according to the needs of the story. Fergie was killed in the silo and McFee right outside of it. And that left Paul.

The killing of Paul went through innumerable changes. At one point, Samuel shot him. This was quickly rejected, believing that audiences wouldn't sympathize with this act by a child. Then Rachel shot him. Later, Rachel rang the bell. But each of these solutions made Rachel the active character who caused the climax to happen, rather than the main character, John Book.

Then it was decided that the Amish would come and surround Paul, separating him from John. In rehearsals, this didn't work. Finally, the solution emerged—Samuel rings the bell, and the Amish come forward to "bear witness."

THE EDITING PHASE

Thom Noble won the Academy Award for Best Editing. He was not the first editor on the job. Another had already tried to cut the film, but there was disagreement over the direction it was taking. Thom was then bought on board to see if he could make it work.

Many of the cuts I mentioned were made by Thom. He and Peter agreed that the story should move quickly from the set-up at the Amish farm to the city scenes, and then move quickly back to the Amish farm. That meant cutting any scenes in Act One that weren't absolutely essential to the story, and it meant that the story kept moving in Act Two. Thom's ability to tighten the story and pace the story, while preserving the lyricism, made the film work. As Bill Kelley said, "Thom got the pace right, and that made all the difference."

SUMMARY

I asked Bill if there were any areas where he felt that the writers lost out. He mentioned that there were three elements he fought for, and he won on two of them. He felt that it was necessary for three men, not one, go after John in Act Three. He also insisted on the scene about shunning when Eli confronts Rachel after her dance with John. Both of these remained in the film. But Bill had one other wish. He wanted to show more of the good-bye between John and Rachel at the end. He suggested that Rachel give John her husband's hat, which would be a gift and would acknowledge their relationship. Bill also felt that this gift exchange would imply the possibility that they might see each other again. Instead, Peter chose to play the scene as a non-verbal good-bye.

This rewrite process was unique in some ways. There were no big disagreements between the creative team. Ed Feldman and David Bombyk felt strongly about protecting the integrity of the script, so most changes tightened the story or textured the story rather than changed it. About ninty percent of the original script remained essentially the same, even after considerable rewriting. The early drafts of the script were already well-structured and clear. So most of the changes were creative changes rather than structural changes.

The film did very well critically and commercially. It made about $100 million in theatrical release, not counting video rentals and sales, which would add considerably to that figure. Almost every review of the film was favorable. It received eight Academy Award nominations and two Academy Awards, for Best Original Screenplay and for Best Editing.

This is no surprise, considering that the film began with a strong and workable script. Each act is strong, with turning points that move us from act to act. The use of barriers and reversals and scene sequences give the story momentum. The character through-lines and character functions are clear. The theme is developed well through contrasts and images and motifs.

The creative team had considerable experience in the film business and knew how to translate these elements into a workable film. Peter Weir's ability to find a directorial approach to the script and Thom Noble's ability to edit and hone and focus the story all worked together to create one of the five best films of 1985.

224

Epilogue

There is no lack of good scripts in Hollywood. Many people write good scripts with an interesting story and memorable characters. But there are few great scripts. A great script leaps off the page and "knocks your socks off." Paramount Studios knew they had a good script with *Witness* and expected it to be nominated for Best Original Screenplay even before the film was made. Three times in my consulting work I have worked with scripts that were so tight, so workable that the only advice I could give the producer or writer was "Don't touch it!"

Making a good script great brings together a combination of skills. The writer needs to have a fresh approach to the subject matter. S/he needs to be original, unique, and creative. The writer needs to have a sense of what appeals to audience and how to tell a good tale. And, the writer needs to know structure, how to execute the story so that it makes sense.

This book has focused on the execution of a script because most films fail for structural reasons. If you read reviews, you'll notice that rarely do they criticize the casting, the directing, or even the subject matter. Usually, reviews criticize structural problems: an unclear storyline, poorly motivated characters, rambling subplots, too many characters, an ending that doesn't fit the beginning, too many unanswered questions at the end. All of these problems are fixable. If they don't work in the writing of the script, they need to be reworked in the rewriting stage.

What I have tried to do in this book is to discuss the underlying concepts that make a workable script. By understanding the craft of writing, you will be in a better position to resolve problems and to have a clearer idea of when your writing is "off track" or "on track." Whether writer, producer, executive, or director, working with these elements can make writing and rewriting easier and can lead to a stronger and more integrated film. Making a good script great is a process. It's a process where the craft of writing and art of writing together create the magic of film.

Index

A

About the Author

Dr. Linda Seger began her script consulting business in 1983. Since then, she has worked with such well-known writers, producers, and companies as Ray Bradbury, Tony Bill, ITC Productions, Charles Fries Entertainment, TriStar Pictures, and the Sundance Institute. She has given seminars for executives at ABC, CBS, and Embassy Television, as well as for the American Film Institute, the Directors Guild of America, the Writers Guild of America, and the Academy of Television Arts and Sciences and Academy of Motion Picture Arts and Sciences. She is married and lives in Venice, California.